Contents

Dedication

For Ruth, and all who stood by her as she was crossing over.

Introduction:
Crossing Over

C rossing over... We might use it as a euphemism for dying, but the metaphor captures an important aspect of what happens. Someone crosses over from this world to the presence of God. There is a departing, a saying "goodbye", a letting go. That is why the French speak of saying *"adieu"* as a *"petit mort"*, "a little death". Death is the big "Goodbye" but not the end.

There is a crossing over to embrace something more, something Beyond, which can be a joyful hope for the believer in the midst of the pain and the tears.

What is Dying?

Bishop Brent (1862–1929), Bishop of the Philippines, wrote the meditation "What is Dying?" This captures the sense of letting go and of arriving at a new place in an excellent way. He imagines a ship setting sail, and the travellers turn to wave at their friends and relatives on the

shore until they get smaller and smaller and smaller. Then they are seen no more. The travellers turn, and there is a new shore, with people waving them on, beckoning them.

What is Dying?

A ship sails and I stand watching till she fades on the horizon, and someone at my side says "She is gone."

Gone where? Gone from my sight, that is all. She is just as large now as when I last saw her. Her diminished size and total loss from my sight is in me, not in her.

And just at the moment when someone at my side says, "She is gone," there are others who are watching her coming, over their horizon and other voices take up a glad shout, "There she comes!"

That is what dying is. An horizon and just the limit of our sight.

Lift us up, Oh Lord, that we may see further.

(Bishop Brent)

1

Surprise!

Our experiences of awe and beauty, of compassion and value point to the reality of God and eternity. This is a great and joyful mystery. It will dawn on us as a wonderful surprise, a joyful gift.

Seeds of Hope

Death sounds like such a morbid topic. I must have become aware of death as a concept when I was about three years old. I remember the occasion very clearly. I was lying on a bed watching my mother chase a wasp around the bay window. Smack! It was gone, splattered over the window pane. "There! It's dead!" she said, satisfied. "What's 'dead'?" I asked, innocently. She paused, a little unsure of herself, and then replied, "Well, it's a bit like going to sleep and never waking up again."

That was scary for a three-year-old to handle, and many today wonder if there might be anything more to dying than that – everlasting sleep. If you are reading this because of a bereavement, the pain will be intense. That cannot be taken away, but perhaps a seed of hope can be born with the help of these pages. Whether carrying a burden of loss, or merely curious, the hope of something that lies beyond the death of the body is a precious and sublime thing. It is about joy and bliss without end. It is far more than sleep.

I remember a friend of mine who lost his father rather suddenly. We had just started at university as undergraduates, and his father had a heart attack. It was, as can be imagined, a huge shock. He was shaken and numb. He went to view the body before the funeral and reported back to me: "It wasn't my dad. He'd gone. It was just a shell." The uniquely precious individual, the personality of the man, had moved on, passed on, crossed over. But to where?

How can we begin? How can we get a handle on this huge concept?

Hints of Eternity

One agnostic woman once asked a Christian a searching question. "You go on about this Jesus," she said. "When I walk on a beach in the sun, and watch the crashing waves, I like to pick up a shell and hold it to my ear. I hear the wonder of the sea. This is beauty. This is spiritual. Is this what you mean by 'Jesus'?"

Christians mean *more* than that, but it's not a bad starting point. To see a glimpse of God in beauty that moves and enchants us is a wonderful gift.

There is an ancient beauty that can be glimpsed in nature, when its sheer beauty or mystery seems to open up and stare at us.

I'm not very proficient with mountains; I prefer walking on the flat. I have accompanied a church group to the English Lake District several times as their chaplain in the past. They scaled the heights as I pottered about below. They came back each evening entranced, moved, stunned by the beauty they had seen in the raw, hanging off rock faces and perching on patches of scrub. I, too, could take in the grandeur from a different angle, seeing the majesty of the towering hills and the seductive mists at play. We used to recite a psalm daily:

> I will lift my eyes to the hills –
> From whence comes my help?
> My help comes from the Lord,
> Who made heaven and earth...   (Psalm 121:1–2)

We were feeling something of what the English poet William Wordsworth called "a sense sublime of something far more deeply interfused". He had this sense of mystified awe when he was transfixed while rowing on Derwentwater in the Lake District. It was just so staggeringly beautiful, and he was so small before it.

Nature can sometimes come alive, almost addressing us and arresting us with its freshness and beauty. I can remember a trip to the Isle of Man with my school when I was about ten years old. We entered one of the glens after a tram ride. The branches covered us; we walked deeper and deeper into it; a splashing, trickling stream, pure enough to drink from, ran through the bottom. Bluebells and flowers sprouted all around, and glimpses of sunlight danced, yes, danced on the water. Ten-year-old boys do not easily stop and look long at the beauty of nature (it is most "uncool"), but this stopped me in my tracks and took my breath away. It was, I think, one of my first experiences of awe.

These experiences are called "hints of transcendence" by theologians; they evoke something greater, a wonder that is timeless. In the moment that we stop and have our breath taken away, it is as though all time stands still. That time-lessness is an echo of eternity, a nostalgia for heaven. As the poet William Blake put it in his *Auguries of Innocence*:

> To see a world in a grain of sand
> And a heaven in a wild flower,
> Hold infinity in the palm of your hand
> And eternity in an hour.

Perhaps our own experiences can whisper to our hearts that there is something after this life. Such moments of stunning awe and beauty make time stand still and they slit open a crack into eternity.

An Awesome World

The author Douglas Coupland, in *Life After God*, describes a car journey with a child: "Just after you saw the eagle you asked me, seemingly out of the blue, 'Where do people come from?' I wasn't sure if you meant the birds and bees or if you meant the ark or what have you. Either direction it was a tad too much for me to handle just then, but you did get me to thinking. I mean, five thousand years ago people emerge out of nowhere – *sproing!* – with brains and everything and begin wrecking the planet. You'd think we'd give the issue more thought than we do."

How often do we think about that?

Cosmologists have coined the term "the *anthropic* principle". Put simply, this states that the universe exists in such a way as to allow *us* to exist. The universe can be comprehended and studied by human beings not only because it is constructed in a manner open to human reason, but because *it allows us to be*. As Stephen Hawking says in his best-selling *A Brief History of Time*, "Why is the universe the way we see it? The answer is then simple: if it had been different, we would not be here!"

What it is easy to forget is that this state of being is so finely tuned. If a few things were different, we would not have a universe that could support human life. If the earth were a fraction closer to or further away from the sun, for example, it would be impossible. Also, the universe expands, and contains gravity, which acts as a brake. The expansion comes from the "Big Bang", from a primeval explosion of a microscopic ball of matter. If the expansion was slightly greater, then the galaxies could not form; if gravity was slightly greater, then everything would collapse in on itself. In order to have structure, and life-supporting structure, we need to balance the forces to within 1 part in 10 to the power of 60, or, 1 followed by sixty zeros. This is like the odds against hitting a target one centimetre square on the other side of the universe!

The human brain is itself a marvel of engineering. Marian Diamond said, "The brain is a three-pound mass you can hold in your hand that can conceive of a universe a hundred-billion light years across." Raymond Keene, in an article in the English magazine *The Spectator*, offered the following impressive statistics:

> Your brain weighs about the same as a bag of sugar, approximately 2 per cent of body weight, yet the brain alone accounts for up to 20 per cent of your body's energy needs. A million million nerve cells are packed into every (well, almost every) human head and there are as many cells between your ears as there are stars in the Milky Way galaxy. Each of these cells can be connected with up to 1,000,000 others, and just counting each possible nerve connection in the human brain cortex – the outer layer – at the rate of one per second would take 32 million years…

This "Wow!" factor can make us wonder why anything exists at all. The cosmos might not be some great big, accidental, self-replicating machine but a living mystery, a creation.

A kiss is another example. This can be reduced to the bare biology, the mechanics, as "the approach of two pairs of lips, the reciprocal transmission of carbon dioxide and microbes, and the juxtaposition of two orbicular muscles". How does that account for the passion, the fun, the sharing? Materialists see all things as impersonal and mechanical at root, from a Beethoven symphony to the beauty of the pale moonlight.

What if the personal dimension is not a side effect or an illusion but the deepest, most profound layer of reality itself? If this material world is not all that there is, if our minds cannot be reduced down to electrical impulses and chemicals in our brains, then there is the hope of something Beyond.

The Beauty of God

Christians recognise beauty as stemming from God, for St Augustine could pray, "O thou beauty most ancient and with all so fresh." This is the Giver of life, moving, blessing, flowing through all things. As the poet Gerard Manley Hopkins sensed, "there lives a dearest freshness deep down things." This is not to start with a hypothetical being *out there* somewhere, but a radical and ultimately personal *depth* to life. Right here, in *this life*, we sense something transcendent, mysterious and wonderful.

Experience of this world opens up depths, possibilities and teasing insights, and involves transcendent moments. This world, all down here, is more mysterious, many-layered, and spiritual, than materialists would allow. There is so much within that points further down and out and beyond. It is not just about postulating a "maybe world", an imaginary land in the sky. What we sense here suggests there is more than the material.

Faith *is* possible; faith can come alive; faith can be nurtured. Faith means "trust", trust in things that you cannot see for certain. Looking at a baby's smile, staring into the eyes of a lover, or watching the stars glisten in the night sky, fading away into infinity…all these things can help us trust.

The young woman with the seashell to her ear linked

the beauty she heard with Jesus. Christians see what God is like supremely in Jesus of Nazareth, in that striking Man of compassion. He showed, above all, that the path of self-giving love was what turned the universe, deeper than sub-atomic, quantum physics.

But what of death and dying, of mourning and of hope? A God who creates such an intricate and marvellous universe, who pours himself into Jesus, who is reflected in the love in our hearts and the breathtaking timelessness of the sunrise, can be trusted. There is something more; there is something Beyond. It will be a surprise.

It's a Surprise!

Waiting for a surprise is enchanting. Infuriating at times, frustrating, causing rising impatience, but it is a wonderful thing. When my children were younger, they did not have much idea of what might come their way at Christmas. It was a delight to plan what to give them, searching around, picking up bargains and interesting items that we thought would enthral them. Later on, the list of "wants" all but demolished this older awe.

I can look back to my own childhood and recall the joyful surprise when I encountered my Christmas presents – huge things, things I had never expected. That was a long time ago!

Mystery tours are not as enticing; in the south of England they usually end up at Windsor or in Brighton, but they are fun. For the young child they are more adventurous. I can think of one little girl who kept asking where she was going. Her daddy took her to the circus, her first ever visit. The laughter, the colours, the clowns and the animals made a lasting impression. This was JOY.

Joy is more than being happy; it is something deeper that bubbles up and lasts longer. It often comes as a surprise. C.S. Lewis wrote about being "surprised by joy" and gave many examples, such as seeing a brilliantly coloured bush when younger. When we think of the afterlife, it is a big mystery. It is something beyond, out of our experience and bigger than the limits of our imaginations. Scriptures and hymns speak of it in endless suggestive symbols. It is transcendent, beyond us. Some say that they cannot imagine how such a thing could work; not being able to imagine something does not mean that it does not exist. It is simply beyond.

The Bible has many things to say about an afterlife, and this book will explore these ideas. The centre of the Christian faith is Jesus, and the belief that God became man in him. The Beyond came in amongst us. He told us something about the spiritual realm that we could not find on our own. But Christians believe that God had been speaking about this for some time through holy men and prophets, dreamers and visionaries who line the pages of the Hebrew Scriptures, the Old Testament part of the Bible. We are given glimpses, hints, assurances and no exact map of the terrain. That is enough. We can hold God's hand and step into the darkness, confident that he will lead us to light – however it works.

Holding God's Hand

Now when Jesus had crossed over again by boat to the other side, a great multitude gathered to Him; and He was by the sea. And behold, one of the rulers of the synagogue came, Jairus by name. And when he saw Him, he fell at His feet and begged Him earnestly, saying, "My little daughter lies at the point of death. Come and lay Your hands on her, that she may be healed, and she will live." So Jesus went with him, and a great multitude followed Him and thronged Him.

While He was still speaking, some came from the ruler of the synagogue's house who said, "Your daughter is dead. Why trouble the Teacher any further?"

As soon as Jesus heard the word that was spoken, He said to the ruler of the synagogue, "Do not be afraid; only believe." And He permitted no one to follow Him except Peter, James, and John the brother of James. Then He came to the house of the ruler of the synagogue, and saw a tumult and those who wept and wailed loudly. When He came in, He said to them, "Why make this commotion and weep? The child is not dead, but sleeping."

And they ridiculed Him. But when He had put them all outside, He took the father and the mother of the child, and those who were with Him, and entered where the child was lying. Then He took the child by the hand, and said to her, "Talitha, cumi," which is translated, "Little girl, I say to you, arise." Immediately the girl arose and walked, for she was twelve years of age. And they were overcome with great amazement. But He commanded them strictly that no one should know it, and said that something should be given her to eat.   (Mark 5:21–24, 35–43)

The story of Jairus' daughter is a moving little human tale in the Gospels. In the midst of ethics and lofty teaching, Jesus goes into the house of a mourning family and bends down beside a bed. He reaches out and touches the hand of a little girl. He calls to her, and her spirit hears. She follows the Good Shepherd and life returns to her body. Her waking vision was of that face, bent low, etched with compassion, aglow with resurrection power, smiling God's smile over her. She did not know what was happening; she did not understand all the theology. She was simply in the presence of Jesus.

Jesus, a name that for some is only a swear word; Jesus, a plaster image for some or an unsmiling face on a window; Jesus, a faded memory of formal church – old hymn books and musty kneelers, maybe.

This is not the Jesus who moves through the pages of the four Gospels – a man full of life, of spirit, that affected all those whom he met, touched, spoke with, prayed with. He left his mark upon them all, a mark of fire and love, of God bursting forth from his beating heart.

One photographer, Mike Gough, dreamed up a crazy project one summer. He got an actor, Barry Richardson, to dress up as Jesus – the usual image of long hair, beard, white robe and blanket over shoulder. Barry walked around central London while Mike filmed the reactions. It was an experiment. There were glances, giggles, awkward silences, and the usual blank faces on the London Underground. Some youths mocked and bowed at Barry's feet, saying, "We're not worthy!" But the striking thing was how the poor and dispossessed, those at the fringes of society, had a kind word. A punk hugged Barry and chatted. A brothel-keeper met his gaze and shivered. It appears that she kept an old, traditional picture of Jesus beside her bed – the only possession of her mother's she had. When Barry looked straight at her, it was like the man in the picture. She felt known. Then there was the old woman, homeless, drunken, filthy. She sat in a tunnel leading to Hyde Park, shouting and cursing. This went on until Barry came within about 25 feet. She became quieter, and then completely shut up, picking up her belongings and scurrying off in silence. What was it that had disturbed her?

This experiment revealed that the figure of Jesus sums up so much for so many, that the compassion of God reaches out to those who know they are broken. As the late bishop and theologian John Robinson once put it, Jesus is "the Human Face of God".

The *real* Jesus is worth following, and he can lead us to eternal life. It is his gift.

Jairus' daughter came back to *this* life; her time was not yet. In a spiritual way, that touch of love, that hand holding ours, can be very real for each of us both in the journey of this life and in the world to come. Just as the little girl mentioned earlier held her daddy's hand and found herself in the circus, so we can find ourselves in the kingdom of heaven. We don't know how it works, how it can be or what exactly it will be like, but following him is enough. He promised, he promises, and calls us to follow.

The afterlife will come as a surprise, and this life and the journey through death are all part of a big Mystery Tour that will be worth the wait.

But as it is written:
"Eye has not seen, nor ear heard,
Nor have entered into the heart of man
The things which God has prepared for those who love Him."   (1 Corinthians 2:9)

It will be a surprise, a surprise full of joy.

2

The History of a Belief

A belief in some kind of after life can be traced back to the dawn of time. It is intrinsically human. It is only in the last couple of centuries that this has been questioned and some find it hard to believe.

Not So Long Ago...

If we are to believe the usual dating schemes for the age of the earth and the cosmos, then human beings, homo sapiens, have not been around for very long – maybe about 100,000 years. This seems like ages and ages, but it has been suggested that if you stand with your arms outstretched and look at the tip of the fingers on the left hand, these will represent the Big Bang and the start of everything. Running down the arm and across the shoulders, when you reach the tip of the fingers on your right hand, this is the point at which homo sapiens emerged. It has not been that long, really.

Humans have always had some form of belief in an afterlife, a desire to live on, a refusal to believe that death is the end. Somehow, our consciousness goes on.

Some today might argue that this is a weakness in our species, a kink of evolution that is programmed into our brains. We are so driven by the need to survive as a species that we dream about going on and on and on. Or, we cannot face the idea of extinction or endless sleep, and thus we make up fantasies and hide behind them like screens to guard our emotions from raw reality.

There is another way of seeing things. Perhaps we are special, more special than all the other creatures on earth, in the sight of the Creator. God has placed in our hearts a desire for him, a longing for heaven, a deep-seated knowledge that we will not simply come to an end. Something new will open up, like the far shore in Bishop Brent's piece mentioned earlier. The Bible says that humans are made in the "image" of God (Genesis 1:26). This is a rich and loaded term. It does not mean that God looks like us; God is Spirit, invisible, beyond matter. It means that we are like God within our minds, within our spirits. We have reason, conscience and creativity, and, above all, we are made to relate to him. We are restless until we do. G.K. Chesterton commented that if we do not believe in God then we will believe in anything. The French philosopher Voltaire quipped, "If God did not exist we would have to invent Him." Deep down, there is a need and a recognition of the existence of God, even if we find it hard to believe intellectually. There's a spark, a yearning inside everyone – somewhere.

Perhaps, with all this in mind, we believe in a life after death because we are designed to live on. We yearn for something that is out there, just as a plant will bend and twist to follow the light, or, out in the desert, it will spread out roots to find water. Life after death then becomes a hope, and not a fantasy. Homo sapiens, though they have been around for a relatively short time in the grand scheme of things, can be considered the joy and crown of creation on earth by God. We are beloved, and we have a destiny.

The Dawn of Time

The earliest known writing is a series of markings on clay tablets that were baked hard to preserve them. The oldest that have been found are from ancient Sumer in the Near East, about 4,000 BC. They are famous for working out a calendar and dates that give us a seven-day week and four seasons to the year. Before this, we only have artefacts, graves and cave paintings. They cannot give us details and stories, only evidence of a belief in something.

The earliest cave paintings seem to record the lifestyle of the hunters, with examples of the animals they preyed upon. There are stick men with spears or arrows, and various handprints, maybe imposed on the rock as a signature. These date back, maybe, to about 40,000 years ago. These paintings might have been used in ritual magic (striking the images to gain power over them) but we can find no trace in their symbols of afterlife ideas. The dead were sometimes buried, and some find clues about a belief in an afterlife in ancient Chinese caves near Beijing.

The first clear proof of an afterlife belief comes when communities of homo sapiens had settled down and had started farming. Then they buried their dead and left things in the graves with the bodies. The earliest known settlement is from 8,000 BC and is Shanidar in Iraq. People were buried in a foetal position, covered in red dye, and with garlands of flowers.

We do not know what they believed in, but the position suggests getting ready for a new birth. Red, a symbol of blood, would have been a symbol of life, of energy. Blood was thought to hold the secret of life for many of the ancients and thus it was a potent force. To cover the body in red suggested that the people were hoping for life to return to it in some way.

Flowers in the graves show compassion and sensitivity, but also hope. Flowers speak of life, of blossom, or new beginnings.

Later centuries reveal similar practices, with bodies buried in the foetal position. Stone tombs such as New Grange in Ireland, or the Long Barrows near Stonehenge in Wiltshire, England, have an opening so that the light of the rising sun will shine straight into the central chamber, bathing the body in light. This is another symbol; a piece of ritual magic maybe, but an expression of hope. There is light beyond the darkness of death.

Putting the objects of the dead – jewellery, weapons, armour, food and drink – with the body, as in the pyramids and Near Eastern tombs, or in pagan Saxon graves, also shows a hope that death was not the end, even if in rather primitive and crude terms. For another, more common, example, at ancient Ras Shamra, on the Syrian coast, the dead were buried under their homes and a funnel fed water down into their graves.

But what did people believe happened to the spirits of the dead?

Hauntings

Perhaps one of the simplest and earliest beliefs was that the spirits of the dead lived on near the grave and around the family. Ancestors had to be honoured and appeased. Offerings were made, and food and drink would sustain them. If they were neglected, they could be a haunting spirit, a malevolent force.

Going Underground

One of the earliest ideas of an afterlife that was written down is of a shadowy world of the dead, the Underworld. Often, this was thought to be literally under the ground, for that was where the dead were placed, after all. Down, down, in the darkness beneath the land of the living, the spirits (often called "shades" or "shadows") of the dead lived in a grey, joyless twilight, remembering their glory days up in the light. The Greek poet Homer mentions this in his epic poems, *The Odyssey* and *The Iliad* (c. eighth century BC) by the name of Hades. The spirits of dead warriors are sent there and it is a joyless existence. In ancient

Near Eastern poetry this place is the "House of Darkness" ruled over by the god Mot ("death"), a place where the sun could not shine. A similar idea is "Sheol", mentioned in the early parts of the Old Testament in the Bible. The Hebrews assumed that the dead lived on in the same way as the Underworld's shades at first, until they realised more truth about the God who had called them and whom they then worshipped. He promised far, far more (but more on this development in the next chapter).

Sometimes there are hints in the old myths that great men and women would have some measure of reward in this miserable Underworld, with special lands or departments where even the sun could shine on them now and again.

Going Up?

There was a heaven also, the world of the gods, such as Mount Olympus for the Greeks. Usually, mortals were not admitted. This was the exclusive club of the immortals, as played out with full dramatic effect in the Disney film *Hercules*. If Hercules gains mortality to be able to freely love someone, he must forfeit his place with the gods. There were exceptions, though. Outstanding individuals were granted admission. We can even see a trace of this in the early part of the Bible. Enoch was taken before he died to be with God (Genesis 5:21–24). Indeed, as belief in an afterlife unfolds in the Bible, we find the daring and original idea that God will welcome his people into the bliss of heaven.

The ancient Near Eastern poem *Gilgamesh* is the first story that we know of to be written down on clay tablets, around 4,000 years ago. It is a thunderingly good adventure and fantasy tale of a hero who was semi-divine. It is far more than an adventure story about a king who slays men and monsters, though. It is a heart-rending quest for immortality. Gilgamesh travels to the Underworld after the death of a dear friend to learn the secret of immortality. He searches for the legendary Utnapishtim, a Near Eastern version of Noah. Gilgamesh has to cross a sea of death to reach him in a land of the blessed. Utnapishtim was given eternal life *as a gift* by the gods. He and his wife were the survivors of the great flood. Gilgamesh is sent home, being told that such a gift is not for him, but there is a magic plant deep under the water. This can give eternal life. Gilgamesh searches and finds it. He rises to the surface and celebrates, but a snake eats it and gains the power of shedding its skin and renewing itself. So, immortality evades humanity again, slipping out of Gilgamesh's hands. (Note how a serpent is seen as a symbol of evil and the enemy of humanity here, as in the Book of Genesis.)

Going to a Land of the Blessed?

In ancient Egypt, the pyramids began life very simply as square stone tombs called *mastabas*, from the word for a bench. The Step Pyramid of Pharaoh Djoser in about 3,000 BC was a series of *mastabas* built upon each other, in decreasing size. Later pyramids filled in the steps to form sloping sides. They were burial chambers for the rulers, housing servants and artefacts for the afterlife. Many of the hieroglyphic inscriptions speak only of the pharaoh and the hope of his rebirth in a spiritual form. The Egyptian god Osiris was the Lord of the Dead as he had been killed and raised up again. Through the power of Osiris, with various priestly rituals and star alignments, the pharaoh could rise again. Mummification was a mark of respect for the body of the deceased when it developed in the later Egyptian kingdoms. However, it does not seem that the Egyptians believed that the actual body would rise again, but that a spiritual form of it would.

Various Egyptian beliefs can be traced at different times in their history. The oldest have offerings and artefacts in common graves, with special attention given to the pharaoh. Gradually, the belief emerges that each person has a soul that separates from the body at death. This soul is in two parts, the Ba and the Ka. The Ba is a winged being, a soul bird which could move through the heavens. The Ka is the personality of the deceased. The soul would be judged by Osiris in the Underworld and if good deeds outweighed bad deeds, then it would be taken into Osiris' kingdom, a sort of Underworld Egyptian society where life went on pretty much as before. At least this was not dull and gloomy! The condemned were thrown to the mercy of demonic monsters. (Similar ideas of divine judgment and weighing of souls can be found in the ancient religion of Zoroastrianism from Persia [now Iran]. There, the soul has to pass over a bridge; if it is righteous, the way becomes broad and easy to cross. If unrighteous, it becomes narrower and narrower – akin to a stunt in Indiana Jones but with eternal consequences. The righteous entered a land of the blessed that was full of light and health.)

Speaking Philosophically...

The Greek philosophers, such as Plato (428–347 BC), taught a blend of afterlife ideas which had moved on from the Hades of Homer. The philosophers believed that a purified, rational soul could leave this world behind and join with heavenly Light, Reason or God. The great philosophers of the fifth century onwards were working towards a concept of monotheism, even if a rather abstract one.

Less developed souls would go through a period of judgment and purification in the Underworld, or would be reincarnated. The idea of "the transmigration of souls" or reincarnation seems to have entered Greece in the sixth century BC with teachers such as Pythagoras (c. 580–500 BC), who was an excellent mathematician and a mystic. The belief had probably travelled from the Far East.

Coming Back Again

Belief in reincarnation – being born on earth again – probably began in India. The earliest texts that speak of it are the classical Hindu scriptures, the *Vedas* (c. 1500–900 BC). This is taught again and again in other Hindu holy books, especially the popular meditation the *Bhagavad Gita*, "The Song of God":

> As a man leaves an old garment and puts on one that is new, the spirit leaves his mortal body and then puts on one that is new. (*Bhagavad Gita* 2:22)

Samsara is the name given to the endless round of rebirths until a person's soul is pure enough to find release, *moksha*. This release is a joining with God, understood either in a personal sense, or in an impersonal sense of merging with Light. There are different views in Hinduism.

The soul gathers a tradition or force of deeds, both good and bad, negative and positive, called *karma*. *Karma* decides a person's fate, what they are reborn as.

Reincarnation is an integral part of the belief system of Hinduism, Buddhism and Sikhism.

Belief in reincarnation has become very popular in the West, giving a comfort and a hope that we can live again and that death is not the end. It is a warm and fuzzy idea, though, which is often ignorant of the tenets of Eastern philosophy and the whole cycle of rebirth and the purification that must be undertaken. It must be asked if there really is any real comfort, either, in the notion that we are reborn with no recollection of who we have just been. It is as though the "you" that a person is now is as good as dead, or is asleep for aeons until *moksha* is finally achieved.

Sometimes evidence is adduced for reincarnation from memories of past lives. These are usually the result of hypnosis sessions, where a person is asked to regress in age and memories as far as they can. Many colourful descriptions and stories can emerge of life in ancient Egypt or whatever. They cannot be substantiated and are probably the product of our imaginative faculties, the same faculty that makes us dream. Now and then, a story is told that can be checked, and names and dates tally. The problem is that the human brain can store vast amounts of information in the memory banks. Details that we have read can pop in there and be used again in hypnotic sessions without us realising it. We would not necessarily recall having heard the information earlier.

There are other practices, such as the manner in which a new Dalai Lama is chosen. The artefacts of the deceased leader are taken around the villages of Tibet until a child steps forward who knows how to put them on in the correct manner. He is thought to be a reincarnation of the former Master. Intriguing, but there might be many types of extrasensory perception possible, even with the departed.

Occult forces might also be at work to make links that are beyond our normal powers.

It cannot be stressed enough that reincarnation is just one form of afterlife belief and it is *not* Christian. It is not in the Bible at all and the great creeds of the church do not teach it. This does come as a surprise for some people. The Bible teaches resurrection, a concept that will be unpacked in later chapters.

Some might argue that when Jesus taught that people are to be "born again" (John 3:3) he was teaching reincarnation. This is most assuredly not so. A careful reading of that passage shows that Jesus was using a metaphor for spiritual birth, for inner transformation and a new beginning. The Greek actually says "born from above", i.e. from the Spirit of God. The idea of a new birth as a metaphor of spiritual renewal is picked up in 1 Peter 1:3. This clearly does not mean reincarnation, either.

Once You're Dead, You're Dead?

There were occasional voices that questioned any idea of post-mortem existence among ancient thinkers, such as the Greek philosopher Democritus (460–370 BC). He thought that death was the end. Full stop. Period. This scepticism did not catch on until the last few centuries, however. It began with a movement known as the Enlightenment in the eighteenth century. It can be summed up in the words of atheistic thinker Bertrand Russell in the twentieth century: "When I die, I rot." The Enlightenment was the time when the scientific method was being worked out, and what could be observed with the five senses, what could be touched and measured, was most real and reliable. There was an urge to shake off the control of the church and much superstition from the Middle Ages. As usual, thinkers tend to overreact in such circumstances.

The materialist position is that the mind is simply the brain working, as superbly explained by scientists such as Stephen Pinker, who works for MIT, the Massachusetts Institute of Technology, pioneering methods of artificial intelligence.

> The mind is a system of organs of computation, designed by natural selection to solve the kinds of problems our ancestors faced in their foraging way of life.
>
> (*How the Mind Works*)

In more recent years, others are not so sure. There is a searching, agnostic position that recognises what we do not know as much as what we do. There is a place for mystery and awe. The whole is greater than the sum of the parts, and if a symphony is more than sounds and electrical impulses in the brain, or a kiss more than an exchange of microbes and air, then the thinking mind might be more than the physical brain. How this consciousness might survive the death of the brain is anyone's guess, but it is an open question. Perhaps the mind is formed from the wondrous workings of the brain, but it is greater than the sum of its parts, and will somehow survive physical death. Or maybe the brain is like a TV set that acts as a transmitter or receiver for the mind.

> Consciousness brings the mind alive; it is the ultimate puzzle to the neuroscientist. It is your most private place. This ultimate puzzle, the subjective experience of consciousness, is perhaps a good place for any purely scientific survey, namely one of objective facts, to cease.
>
> (Dr Susan Greenfield, *The Human Brain: A Guided Tour*)

This position is akin to the shocked statement of my friend who lost his father and went to look at the body: "It wasn't my dad. He'd gone. It was just a shell."

What is the "I" in my head, and where does it go?

There is a move away from Enlightenment certainties, recognising that such thinkers often threw the baby out with the bathwater. There is a spiritual openness, a thirst, a searching for belief and hope that takes shape in the many ideas of the New Age movement. There is a fascination with spirit/ghost stories and with angelic presences and channelling spirits of the dead. The latter is warned against in the Bible as being spiritually dangerous; more of that in the next chapter. There is also a growth in interest in what are known as Near Death Experiences (or NDEs).

Near Death Experiences

NDEs describe the conditions experienced by a patient who nearly dies, usually during surgery, and returns to life by being resuscitated. There is a common pattern of feeling that they are floating above their bodies, and a tunnel opens up with a bright light at one end. In the light, they might see friends, gardens, or Jesus/an angel/a Being of Light. I recall speaking to someone who had had one of these back in the 1970s. He used to ride a motorbike and he had been in a crash. He lay on the hospital trolley in deep pain. He sensed that his spirit left his body and went into a tunnel of light and stood before Jesus. It was not time for him to pass over and he was sent back. He remembers the sensation of the pain as he re-entered his body. This man was a committed Christian, and he would have expected to meet Jesus in such circumstances.

Another story is about a businessman who was on a

trip to Australia in 1986. He had a heart attack and was in a coma for two and a half weeks:

> I was detached from my body and was looking down on myself. Then I was taken by the hand into a really beautiful garden... At the end was a gate, and a voice said I had to go through it back to my body. I felt so peaceful that I didn't want to go, but the voice insisted...

He saw himself being pushed on a trolley as he entered his body again. The porters said that they had remembered him laughing during this time, and wondered what was going on!

NDEs were first reported by psychiatrist Raymond Moody in Virginia in 1965, after he had heard George Ritchie tell his story.

As a young soldier in 1943, Ritchie was stationed in Texas in the USA. He had a few hours to get to Virginia by train. Then he could continue his medical studies and be discharged from the army. The problem was that he had contracted double pneumonia. He slowly slipped into unconsciousness and was aware of leaving his body and rising above it in his hospital room. Then he went speeding through the air in his spirit form. He looked down and saw a bridge which he had never seen before. He was frightened and called out to God for help. Then he was in the corner of his room again, above his body. A bright light filled the room and a Being of Light stood before him. He instinctively bowed down. He knew it was Jesus as the words, "Stand up, you are in the presence of the Son of God" flooded into his mind. He described the Being as "the most magnificent being I have ever known..." and he saw images of his past life flash before him: "An astonishing love. A love beyond my wildest imagining. This love knew every unlovable thing about me – the quarrels with my stepmother, my explosive temper, the sex thoughts I could never control, every mean, selfish thought and action since the day I was born – and accepted and loved me just the same."

Later, he was to realise that the bridge he had seen corresponded with that at Vicksburg, Mississippi, a bridge he had never visited or seen before, as far as he knew.

After talking to Ritchie, Dr Moody went on to collect some 150 cases. These were followed by Kenneth Ring, a social psychologist from Connecticut, publishing his methodical research in 1980. Then, a paediatrician from Seattle, Dr Melvin Morse, collected many stories from children. In the UK, a neurophysicist, Dr Peter Fenwick, collected more than 300 examples. People seemed to have these more frequently than was realised, and they did not say anything for fear of ridicule in a materialistic society. Perhaps people have far more spiritual feelings than they are prepared to speak about. Such things are intensely personal for many. Other researchers have followed, and individuals have written books or sold magazine articles about their personal story. People really do experience something, and it affects them afterwards. They feel more sensitive, generous and grateful, and less fearful of death. Some, but not all, turn to religion. A few become very sensitive to ghostly presences in hauntings.

But is This Proof?

Convinced materialists like Susan Blackmore, a psychiatrist from the University of the West of England in Bristol, offer other explanations. In her book *Dying to Live* she collects many typical stories, but tries to explain these by the chaos sparked off in the cerebral cortex of the brain as the brain is dying. A mixture of endorphins and oxygen starvation might account for the tunnels, the sense of being out of the body and the bright lights. The people see what they expect to see, such as comforting scenes from their memory banks, as with a middle-aged woman who saw her own garden and met her recently deceased friend. Or, if Christian, they see Jesus. Blackmore is very biased, it must be said, and she is guilty of wanting not to believe as much as some might be of wanting to believe. She does seem to ignore the lasting effects upon NDE claimants, and the differences between their feelings and those of people who know they are drug-affected, hallucinating or oxygen-starved. But, then again, Blackmore challenges people to come up with hard evidence.

What Sort of Evidence Could There Be?

The only possible thing is when people claim to come out of their bodies, they might see something that they could not have known about, as Ritchie claimed about the bridge.

Here are some typical stories: an old man who saw a nurse place his false teeth in a cupboard when he was in a coma. Another is about a woman in a cancer clinic describing a letter a woman was writing to her husband in a different room. This was exactly as she had described when they went to look. Blackmore would argue that these are too flimsy – they are based on personal testimony and hearsay. Often, the people in the stories have moved on and cannot always be traced to confirm events. She looks for controlled experiments.

Professor Christopher French of Goldsmith's College,

London is sceptical too, but he does acknowledge that we do not really know what might be happening and that NDEs are striking experiences:

> I think it will be a long time before we fully understand the NDE, but it is an incredibly fascinating and profound experience for the people that have it and it would certainly be a mistake for science to close its eyes towards those kinds of experience.

A final thought, here, is that people who have suffered hallucinations, or oxygen starvation, act very differently from those who have experienced NDE. George Ritchie now works as a psychologist with people who have hallucinations, and he feels that these experiences are markedly different from his own. There is at least one case of a former pilot who suffered oxygen starvation and, later, an NDE. He has described the sense of disorientation in the aircraft, and told how pilots tried to land on clouds. Yet the NDE was sharp, clear, and totally different in feel. These experiences also change the experient, having a lasting effect. Crazy brains and hallucinations do not usually do that.

This is also the view of Penny Sartori, who has conducted research at Morriston Hospital: "I documented twelve cases of people who had had hallucinations and I found that the hallucinations were very different from the NDE." She pointed out that hallucinations tend to be more random and jumbled, like dreams.

Where to Now?

Religions might have their insights after all. When we trawl through them we see a belief that the soul survives the death of the body. There are ideas of being born a second time, and ideas of going underground, plus ideas of being raised up spiritually into a place of bliss (whether a special land or heaven itself). What is it, and where is it, that NDE experients might be visiting?

We need to turn now to the Bible, starting with the Old Testament, and the God who gradually revealed himself to the ancient Israelites. He has something much more original, substantial and exciting to promise than the many theories of past tribes and nations, or the speculations of the New Agers today.

3

The Old Testament Hope

The Old Testament was written over hundreds of years. We can trace a development of faith and insight as the plan of God was revealed, step by step. A clear belief in an afterlife emerged in the form of the resurrection of the dead.

The Torah

The five books of Moses – Genesis, Exodus, Leviticus, Numbers and Deuteronomy – form the books of the Torah or Law. These are the most sacred parts of the Scriptures for Jews to this day. They contain the 613 laws plus various stories of the ancestors of the Jews and the escape from Egypt, led by Moses. In modern synagogues, the scrolls of the Torah are placed in a special container, the ark, at the front of the building as a focal point. They are carried out and around the synagogue at times in joyful procession.

There is nothing directly in these pages about an afterlife. For this reason, one party of the Jews, the Sadducees, refuted any afterlife hope at the time of Jesus. God's promises were seen by them for this life and for their children. However, there are some foundational truths in the Torah which the whole of the afterlife hope is built upon.

(a) The Image of God

In Genesis 1:26 human beings are made in the image and likeness of God. In Genesis 2:7 the same idea is presented as God breathing spirit into Adam, formed from the ground. The book of Genesis affirms that there is a special touch and gift of God in the human spirit. We are more than animals; we are blessed with spirituality. I recall a visit to a zoo as a child. I was captivated by the antics of a gorilla. It showed intelligence and made gestures at us. Then I looked into its eyes. They were dull and shallow compared to those of a human; I felt a spark was lacking, for all its animal sophistication.

What happens to that spark, that spirit, is not mentioned in the Torah, but it must return to God as our bodies return to the dust.

(b) Eden and the Tree of Life

Genesis 2 and 3 tell the story of the earthly paradise, Eden. In the midst of this is the Tree of Life. This would bestow immortality, but Adam and Eve ignore this in favour of a different tree which brings a curse. Eden is closed off from them and they lose the Tree of Life. A hope of immortality was right there for the first people. There is a hope in the Old Testament that Eden will be restored, as we shall see, and a prophecy of redemption in Genesis 3:15 when the seed of the woman will crush the serpent, predicting the victory of Jesus over Satan. The details are not spelt out, but there will be a reversal of the fall, a restoration of what has been lost, including the gift of the Tree. Whether some see the Tree as symbolic of spiritual truth and eternal life or as a literal, blessed tree, the promise of immortality is there.

(c) Covenant

The Torah introduces the idea of the covenant with God. Covenants were solemn, binding agreements in the ancient Near East. Kings made them with each other to make peace. God made a covenant with his people, first of all with Abraham when he promised him many descendants (see Genesis 15), and with Moses, binding the Hebrews to his service out of gratitude for their deliverance from slavery in Egypt (Exodus 19). It was unheard of for God to make a covenant, promising to protect his people. It was an act of love and condescension.

The covenant is the foundation of the hope of rescue from death; God would not leave his people in the world of the dead (Sheol). One German scholar, Walter Eidrocht, stated that the people of Israel had to go through death to prove that God was faithful to his promises. God was bound to his people in this life and in the world to come. Gradually, they came to realise this.

(d) The God of the Patriarchs

God reveals himself as "the God of Abraham, Isaac and Jacob" at various points in the Torah. A strong hint can be seen in this that these heroes of faith are not dead and gone, lost and just a memory. They live on in the presence of God. Jesus argued this to the Sadducees.

(e) The Power of Life and Death

Deuteronomy 32:39 suggests that God has the power of life and death:

> ... there is no God besides Me;
> I kill and I make alive;
> I wound and I heal...

The phrase "to kill and to make alive" could imply some level of belief in an afterlife as a gift from God.

(f) Enoch

The patriarch Enoch was taken to be with the Lord without dying:

> And Enoch walked with God; and he was not, for God
> took him.   (Genesis 5:24)

To the ancient Hebrews this probably sounded like the stories in the pagan myths about selected individuals, great heroes, being given immortality and allowed to join the gods. If we read this verse in the context of the whole Bible, we see this in a very different light. God's heart is to welcome his people into his presence, and Jesus has opened the way for all to enter. True, Enoch's translation – body and soul into heaven – was outstanding and remarkable, but heaven is open for all. There was one other case of this exceptional entry into glory in the Bible and that concerns the prophet Elijah (2 Kings 2:11–12). Theirs was a different mode of entry, but others can stand in the glory after they have died and their spirit has crossed over. This is not revealed, explicitly, in the pages of the Torah, though. The seeds of this hope are scattered throughout it, as we have seen.

The World of the Dead

The early Old Testament writings are peppered with references to Sheol, the Underworld. "Sheol" is sometimes translated as "the grave", "death" or "the depths". We learn very little information about this place, unlike the picturesque descriptions in ancient Near Eastern myths. The good and the bad both go there (Genesis 37:35; Numbers 16:30); life is a shadow of its former self (Ecclesiastes 9:10); the dead might know something of the state of the living (Isaiah 14:10–11); social status is removed when in Sheol (Job 21:2–26). There are petitions to be delivered from its gates, such as:

> The sorrows of Sheol surrounded me;
> The snares of death confronted me.
> In my distress I called upon the Lord,
> And cried out to my God;
> He heard my voice from His temple,
> And my cry entered His ears.   (2 Samuel 22:6–7)

God rescues someone from death/Sheol, but is there hope in Sheol itself? That idea only emerges as a possibility later on. Some verses seem to despair:

> The dead do not praise the Lord,
> Nor any who go down into silence.   (Psalm 115:17)

King Saul is cursed for disobeying God and seeking the services of a medium. He asks the witch of Endor to bring up the shade of Samuel the prophet from Sheol (1 Samuel 28:1–25). The spirit really seems to be that of Samuel, disturbed from his rest, and he rebukes the king for his disobedience and for meddling with occult practices such as necromancy (contacting the spirits of the dead). Interestingly, the Israelites were forbidden to use mediums or to channel spirits (Deuteronomy 18:10–12). This was abominable to the Lord and was spiritually dangerous. Such things were seen as forbidden zones, and are for Christians today. For someone with little faith or none, it is perfectly understandable why the services of a medium might be sought in the case of a bereavement. People are devastated and they dearly miss the beloved. It is a searing pain of loss and longing. Any possibility of holding on to them, of making contact, is going to be grabbed at. Yet, this is forbidden in the Bible. Besides the possibility of charlatans abusing the vulnerable, we might be getting in touch with anything but the spirit of the deceased loved one. It is like playing with spiritual fire, opening up a portal that should not be opened. Even if the spirit of the loved one can be contacted (and this is debatable), it is forbidden. Things should be left undisturbed. Once we have crossed over, we have crossed over. Despite the stern condemnations of necromancy or spiritualism in the Bible,

God is a God of mercy and forgiveness, especially for those who have dabbled in such dangerous waters in ignorance. If this has been your experience, simply turn to him, and ask his forgiveness and cleansing from any fears or spiritual disturbance that might have resulted from such dabblings.

Leaving aside the issues surrounding contacting the spirits of the dead, the above passages make it clear that there was an early belief that the dead lived on, but it was hardly about being "in glory".

A Digression about Hauntings and Spirits

As contact with the spirits of the dead has been raised, it might be worth considering a few modern examples and the prayerful Christian response to them. Such encounters do seem to happen, though there are hoaxes and overactive imaginations. For example, I heard of one priest who was called out to a home that was supposed to be haunted by the spirit of Elvis. He was rather sceptical, but he did his duty and visited. The living room was filled with Elvis photos and memorabilia – which added to his scepticism. It was late November, and he was told to sit and wait, with the lights out, and Elvis would materialise and walk across the fireplace. They waited, and chatted, and the priest noticed, out of the corner of his eye, a car coming along the street. The light from its headlamps splashed across the darkened room and went right across the fireplace. The couple shot up, "There! There! That's him! It's Elvis!" They had seen what they wanted to see.

Laying aside silly stories like this one, there are inexplicable events which seem to occur frequently. Christian ministers have many stories to tell about hauntings. They are called out to aid a family who are hearing noises or seeing apparitions. This might even be in a newly built house, though this will be on the site of an older building or a site of a murder or a burial ground. A typical story would involve footsteps when no one was there, maybe drawers opening and occasionally voices or breathing. My own experience in the Church of England shows that this is taken seriously enough to have diocesan advisers. Priests are advised to say blessing prayers and to sprinkle holy water at first; if this does not suffice, then the priest will try to find out if a person died there in the past. A requiem mass will be held and this person will be named during the communion. These services are now referred to as rituals of "Laying to Rest". I will give some brief examples below to whet the appetite.

(a) A Phantom Cat

An elderly widow phoned a priest friend of mine and asked him to come round. She lived in a flat in North London, and her cat had recently died. The spot where its basket had been was unusually cold. It felt creepy and strange. My friend walked around the house and confirmed that this was a peculiarly cold spot. The central heating was working fine, and the windows were not draughty. He said some prayers, and sprinkled the spot with holy water. A week later, the lady phoned to say that it had all cleared up.

(b) Violence in the Kitchen

Another priest was once called into a house which was supposed to be haunted and prayers of blessing were said. Nothing happened until they came to the kitchen, when all hell broke loose! He claims that he saw pots and pans flying out of cupboards. He was so disturbed by this that he went outside and lit up! After some research, it seems that a man had committed suicide there. A diocesan expert was called in, and a full requiem was held. The disturbances stopped.

(c) The Haunted Office
Another priest was called into an office block where there were frequent disturbances in one room. Drawers were found open and files were scattered. A strange smell appeared on the stairs and then faded. It reached a point where no one could get into the office, as heavy filing cabinets had been stacked against the door. The point was that the office was several floors up – whoever had done this could not have got out. Again, it was found that a suicide had happened there, and a requiem was held. The trouble ceased.

How do we explain these incidents? They are based upon something, for they are so widespread and so frequent. They form a common pattern, linked to a death. One theory is that they are place memories, as though a place can store emotions or a presence left over from a violent death. An apparition is not then a ghost – i.e. a departed spirit – but a faded spiritual "hologram" of something long ago. This is probably the case if there is no communication with the ghost. If there is movement, speaking and dream encounter, then it might be an actual trapped spirit that has not been able to pass over for some reason, or some other sort of personal, evil spiritual presence, if the encounter is frightening and menacing. Then the full requiem communion service offers them up to the mercy of God and lays something to rest, or exorcism prayers banish any evil presence.

Some Christians would reject any idea that spirits can be trapped, saying that all such things are the work of evil spirits impersonating the deceased. This is debatable, and the example of the spirit of Samuel should remind us that actual contact with the dead might be possible (and biblical!), though something forbidden by God.

The Hope of Glory

Here and there, now and then, a better idea than grey existence in Sheol pops up in the Old Testament Scriptures. This happens in the Psalms, for example:

> … If I make my bed in hell, behold, You are there.
>   (Psalm 139:8)

The king expresses this hope in Psalm 16:10–11:

> For you will not leave my soul in Sheol,
> Nor will You allow Your Holy One to see corruption.
> You will show me the path of life;
> In Your presence is fullness of joy…

Again, Psalm 49:15 says:

> But God will redeem my soul from the power of the grave,
> For He shall receive me.

Psalm 73:24 is stronger still:

> You will guide me with Your counsel,
> And afterward receive me to glory.

Expressions of a hope of being in glory and of seeing God are in the book of Job:

> For I know that my Redeemer lives,
> And He shall stand at last on the earth;
> And after my skin is destroyed, this I know,
> That in my flesh I shall see God
> Whom I shall see for myself,
> And my eyes shall behold, and not another.
>
> (Job 19:25–27)

Job seems to be preaching some form of resurrection!

These beliefs are not well defined. They are clear affirmations that the power of God will deliver from Sheol, though, and that God wants his people to be in his presence. Heaven is to be shared. The driving force for this is probably the belief in God's covenant relationship with Israel. He would not let them go, even in death.

Eden Restored?

One theme which emerges is of a restored paradise on earth. The Garden that was shut off from humanity is opened again and the whole earth is blessed. Ezekiel proclaims this:

> So they will say, "This land that was desolate has become like the garden of Eden…"   (Ezekiel 36:35)

Traces of this can be found in Isaiah's oracles. The blessing that comes from the presence of the Lord is seen in Isaiah 11:6–9, with the wolf lying with the lamb and so on.

Isaiah 26:19 is particularly striking –

Your dead shall live;
Together with my dead body they shall arise.
Awake and sing, you who dwell in dust;
For your dew is like the dew of herbs,
And the earth shall cast out the dead.

Earlier, in Isaiah 25:6–8, there is to be a blessing upon earth from God's holy mountain. Part of this will be plenty to eat, health and prosperity. There will also be an end to death, as we read in verse 8:

He will swallow up death forever,
And the Lord God will wipe away tears from all faces...

The reference to swallowing death is significant, for in Canaanite myths, death (as the god Mot) swallows us up. God is stronger than death, and will defeat it.

Resurrection

The idea of God's visitation on the land, of the dew that brings life, is shown again in Ezekiel's vision of the dry bones (Ezekiel 37:1–14). Here, the Spirit is akin to the dew of Isaiah. This powerful passage describes the raising up of many people. Its primary focus was about the raising up of the nation again after exile to Babylon. The bodies rising are therefore metaphorical, but many Jews took this vision as a prophecy of a hope beyond death also.

The fortress of Masada, just south of the Dead Sea, was held by a group of Jewish Zealots (freedom fighters) from AD 66–73, when it fell to the Romans. Many committed suicide rather than suffer at the hands of the Romans, fearing that they would be cruelly tortured. Archaeologists have discovered skeletons of these people, still clutching old parchment. The parchment is the text of Ezekiel 37 and the vision of the dry bones! It clearly expressed the hope of an afterlife, a resurrection, for them.

We are still with a very physical idea of resurrection. The dead will be raised to new life on an earth that is blessed. One Old Testament reference takes this further. Daniel 12:1–3 describes the resurrection of some to blessing and of some to judgment. Those blessed will be like the stars, a possible heavenly reference, as stars can be seen as symbolic of the angels:

> And many of those who sleep in the dust of the earth
> shall awake,
> Some to everlasting life,
> Some to shame and everlasting contempt.
> Those who are wise shall shine
> Like the brightness of the firmament,
> And those who turn many to righteousness
> Like the stars forever and ever. (Daniel 12:2–3)

Interestingly, the Dead Sea Scrolls contain the idea that the righteous dead will be like the angels, an idea also found in the teaching of Jesus (e.g. Mark 12:25).

This seems to be a more spiritual idea of resurrection than that of Ezekiel or Isaiah; the dead are transformed, not merely raised up again. Scholars suggest that some influence is at play here from the old Persian faith of Zoroastrianism where the dead are judged and some enter a blessed state. Many Jews had been part of the Persian Empire under King Cyrus and afterwards. There might have been a sharing of ideas, and hopes that were developing in the Jewish faith were seen to be similar to those expressed in the ancient faith of their neighbours. This, of course, raises a number of questions about links with other faiths. Perhaps God is not without a witness outside the covenant, but his guidance within it is more pure and sure. Such lofty questions must be left aside for now.

Summing Up

Speculations abounded in the writings of the rabbis between the testaments, and by the time of Jesus various parties had emerged among the Jews. The Sadducees denied the resurrection as a later, new fangled idea that was not in the Torah; the Pharisees championed it. Paul had been a Pharisee and shows that he followed a more sublime, spiritual idea of the resurrection in 1 Corinthians 15:44: "It is sown a natural body; it is raised a spiritual body."

The Old Testament shows a gradual revelation, an unfolding of the heart of God to share his glory and presence with his people. Jesus not only affirmed belief in resurrection, but he was known as the "firstborn from the dead" for he was raised up before anyone else. It is time to turn to the Gospels and his teaching.

4

What Did Jesus Say?

Jesus clearly taught that there was a life after death. He followed the Pharisees and later parts of the Hebrew Scriptures in teaching that there was a resurrection of the dead. He also used vivid symbols to suggest eternal life such as bread or a spring of water. His presence gave out a holy power that touched people with life, forgiveness and healing. Death could not hold him in the end, for he rose again, "the firstborn from the dead". In Jesus we see most clearly what God is like, and what a sure and abiding hope we have.

Little Lamb, Get Up!

In the story of Jairus' daughter, as we saw earlier, Jesus takes the girl by the hand and says (in Aramaic), "Talitha Kum", which means "Little girl, get up!" Life flowed back into the girl (Mark 5:21–24, 35b–43). In his presence was life, and for those whose time was not yet, they were restored to physical life on earth.

There are several similar stories in the Gospels where Jesus raised the dead. These were people who had been dead for a short time – although one, Lazarus, had been wrapped in grave clothes and buried for three days (John 11:38–44). Thankfully, in those days, the bodies were not usually embalmed! The Gospel writers saw these stories as evidence of Jesus' power over death, and in this sense they were prefiguring his own rising. They were not of the same magnitude, though. They were resuscitations – wonderful events, but not transformations. The resurrection of Jesus was far more than life returning to his beaten and battered body; it was a spiritual transformation into a glorious form that could never die again. All the others would one day die; they had simply been revived and had been given longer on earth.

There are occasional stories like these told by Christians throughout the ages, where a believer prays and a recently departed person revives. One recent story is set in Africa, under the ministry of the international evangelist Reinhard Bonnke. He prayed for a pastor who had died and who was laid out awaiting the embalmers. He revived in front of a number of witnesses, including his wife.

Another story was in the UK. A young woman was visiting some friends in a tower block. She wanted to go to one of the top floors, but the lift seemed to stick at the eighth floor. This young woman was a believer, but was feeling downhearted and unsure of her faith at that time. She heard what she could only describe as the audible voice of God, calling her to get out and to go to a flat where someone had just died and to pray for her. She obeyed, in fear and trembling, and as she went along the corridor there were sounds of loud wailing coming from an open door. Friends and distraught relatives crowded around the bedside of a middle-aged woman who had passed away. The Christian young woman entered, gingerly, and asked if she could pray. People nodded and urged her to come in. She prayed for the woman and breath returned to her body. Needless to say, her personal faith was strengthened.

Such stories are rare, and they were not the most common miracle performed even by Jesus, but perhaps a bold reminder that "there are more things in heaven and earth than are dreamed of in our philosophy, Horatio…", to quote Shakespeare's Hamlet.

What is happening? Some comment that in Bible times people did not know as much as we do about the body. Perhaps some conditions that we would now call being in a coma were thought to be death. Did Jesus know this when he said that Jairus' daughter was only sleeping? We do not know. Even today, the body can shut down in various ways, but until there is actual brain death it might be possible for someone to recover, even though to all intents and purposes, otherwise, they have died.

Again, Jesus' reference to Jairus' daughter only sleeping might have been to a Hebrew idea that the spirits of the dead slept until the Day of Judgment, when all would rise again. Jesus had the power of resurrection within him, there and then, as he demonstrated. She was only "sleeping" until touched by him and life returned.

We can go beyond the literal story and the physical scene of Jesus taking her by the hand and calling to her so gently and intimately. We can see a symbol of his dealings with each soul, coaxing them back to life in the afterlife *once* they have crossed over. The God who revealed himself in Jesus is merciful; God is a Christlike God. He has the power to give eternal life, not just to restore life.

Besides his actions, the Gospels present a number of passages where Jesus teaches about the afterlife.

Like the Angels

Then some Sadducees, who say there is no resurrection, came to Him; and they asked Him, saying: "Teacher, Moses wrote to us that if a man's brother dies, and leaves his wife behind, and leaves no children, his brother should take his wife and raise up offspring for his brother. Now there were seven brothers. The first took a wife; and dying, he left no offspring. And the second took her, and he died; nor did he leave any offspring. And the third likewise. So the seven had her and left no offspring. Last of all the woman died also. Therefore, in the resurrection, when they rise, whose wife will she be? For all seven had her as wife."

Jesus answered and said to them, "Are you not therefore mistaken, because you do not know the Scriptures nor the power of God? For when they rise from the dead, they neither marry nor are given in marriage, but are like angels in heaven. But concerning the dead, that they rise, have you not read in the book of Moses, in the burning bush passage, how God spoke to him, saying, 'I am the God of Abraham, the God of Isaac, and the God of Jacob'? He is not the God of the dead, but the God of the living. You are therefore greatly mistaken."   (Mark 12:18–27)

On one occasion in the Gospels, Jesus is tested by a band of Sadducees, who did not believe in the resurrection of the dead (as we saw in the previous chapter). The Sadducees were die-hard traditionalists who saw most of the Old Testament as a new fangled interpretation of the eternal Law given to Moses.

They ask Jesus about a hypothetical situation where a man has seven brothers. He marries and dies, leaving the wife childless. According to their custom, the next brother marries her but dies also, leaving her childless. On and on this goes until all seven die and then she dies. They ask, "In the resurrection, which one is the husband?"

This could have been an honest, heart-searching question by people who were trying to think things through. It could also have been a distraction, an intellectual game to catch Jesus out. He probably detected a mocking, unbelieving spirit behind the question. People can so easily ask awkward question after awkward question to avoid hearing the word of God; faith needs trust, and a leap into the arms of God. We can never work everything out. Faith is trusting what we can't see and what can't be worked out.

Jesus answers that they are trying to understand mysteries, trying to imagine things beyond our ability to understand. Things are different, beyond, transcendent in the resurrection. People are not flesh and blood like now; they do not marry. They are, he says, like the angels. They are spiritual beings, alive in a new level of being. They have moved on and left this order of things behind. What they step into is a mystery and a surprise. Jesus echoes ideas found in the Dead Sea Scrolls where the risen spirits are like the angels. Jesus speaks of two ages: the present age in which people marry, and the age to come where things work differently. The kingdom of heaven is a mystery, beyond our wildest imaginings. It's like when some people ask if there will be golf courses in heaven. The answer is a resounding "No!" because we have to leave everything in this world or this "age" behind and move on to something bigger and better – and many golf widows will say "Amen!" to that! There will be something better, though, and we hang on to what we know until we see something new that wins our hearts. Such is human nature. The letting go of dying is total, a total abandonment into the arms of God and the stream of his life.

Jesus also berates the Sadducees for not knowing their Scriptures and for limiting the power of God. He cleverly finds things in the Torah (the five books of Moses that they did accept as Scripture) that say the dead are not dead to God. When God called himself "the God of Abraham, Isaac and Jacob", this suggested that they were still present to him. They were alive in God. Thus, later ideas about resurrection and the afterlife were present in the early Scriptures, but obliquely so, hinted at rather than clearly expressed.

I AM...

Now Martha said to Jesus, "Lord, if You had been here, my brother would not have died. But even now I know that whatever You ask of God, God will give You."

Jesus said to her, "Your brother will rise again."

Martha said to Him, "I know that he will rise again in the resurrection at the last day."

Jesus said to her, "I am the resurrection and the life. He who believes in Me, though he may die, he shall live. And whoever lives and believes in Me shall never die. Do you believe this?"

She said to Him, "Yes, Lord, I believe that You are the Christ, the Son of God, who is to come into the world."...

Jesus wept. Then the Jews said, "See how He loved him!"

And some of them said, "Could not this Man, who opened the eyes of the blind, also have kept this man from dying?"

Then Jesus, again groaning in Himself, came to the tomb. It was a cave, and a stone lay against it. Jesus said, "Take away the stone." Martha, the sister of him who was dead, said to Him, "Lord, by this time there is a stench, for he has been dead four days."

Jesus said to her, "Did I not say to you that if you would believe you would see the glory of God?" Then they took away the stone from the place where the dead man was lying. And Jesus lifted up His eyes and said, "Father, I thank You that You have heard Me. And I know that You always hear Me, but because of the people who are standing by I said this, that they may believe that You sent Me." Now when He had said these things, He cried with a loud voice, "Lazarus, come forth!" And he who had died came out bound hand and foot with graveclothes, and his face was wrapped with a cloth. Jesus said to them, "Loose him, and let him go." (John 11:21–27, 35–44)

Jesus makes a series of strong statements about himself in John's Gospel. These begin "I am… ". The "I am" is a divine self-reference, linking with the name of God in Exodus 3:14:

And God said to Moses, "I AM WHO I AM". And He said, "Thus you shall say to the children of Israel, 'I AM has sent me to you.' "

The Hebrew is enigmatic, the name being "Yahweh" from which English Bibles derive the word "Jehovah". It is not a personal name but a description, a statement of God's eternal being. Jesus was God incarnate, God in the flesh, filled with divine authority and power.

On one occasion Jesus says, "I am the resurrection and the life." This is when he goes to the tomb of his friend Lazarus. Jesus is overcome with emotion and weeps. Lazarus had been dead for four days, wrapped in grave clothes and sealed up in a tomb. Jesus orders that the tomb be opened. He calls for Lazarus to come out. Lazarus stumbles out, and the people are astonished. They untie him. This is another example of Jesus resuscitating the dead. By saying "I am the resurrection" here, he is proclaiming his power over life and death.

The Bread of Life

And Jesus said to them, "I am the bread of life. He who comes to Me shall never hunger, and he who believes in Me shall never thirst. But I said to you that you have seen Me and yet do not believe. All that the Father gives Me will come to Me, and the one who comes to Me I will by no means cast out. For I have come down from heaven, not to do My own will, but the will of Him who sent Me. This is the will of the Father who sent Me, that of all He has given Me I should lose nothing, but should raise it up at the last day. And this is the will of Him who sent Me, that everyone who sees the Son and believes in Him may have everlasting life; and I will raise him up at the last day."...

I am the living bread which came down from heaven. If anyone eats of this bread, he will live forever; and the bread that I shall give is My flesh, which I shall give for the life of the world."   (John 6:35–40, 51)

Jesus once said "I am the bread of life..." an image of immortal power and sustenance. In the Old Testament the

Hebrews had eaten manna, the "bread from heaven" which they found on the desert floor each morning (Exodus 16). They ate their fill, but were hungry again the next day. Jesus promised that those who ate of his "bread" would live for ever, this being a metaphor of his very self and being. He would raise them up on the last day. Some see a reference to holy communion, the eucharist, in this saying, which there might be. The shared meal that Christians celebrate does speak of the hope of resurrection and eternal life. There, the death and the resurrection of Jesus are proclaimed. One early Christian writer, Ignatius of Antioch, described the communion as "the medicine of immortality". A blessing is found in the sharing of this holy food. Jesus is not absent, but with us though the Holy Spirit.

Living Water

> Jesus answered and said to her, "Whoever drinks of this water will thirst again, but whoever drinks of the water that I shall give him will never thirst. But the water that I shall give him will become in him a fountain of water springing up into everlasting life."   (John 4:13–14)

In John's Gospel, Jesus speaks with a Samaritan woman at a well. He invites her to drink the water that he can give – living water. This will be like a spring welling up inside a believer, a sign of the gift of eternal life here and now that will outlast the death of the physical body. If you have ever studied a spring, it bubbles up and cannot easily be blocked. The water trickles out, forces a way, and shoots up again. I remember playing a game as a child with some friends. We were walking out in the countryside and we came across such a small spring of clear water. We tried pushing stones and pebbles into it but, try as we might, the water just kept on coming. Eternal life with Jesus begins in this life if we receive his gift. It has a quality as well as a longevity. It has a beauty, the beauty and joy of enjoying the presence of God, and "in the presence of the Lord, there is life forevermore".

The Sign of Jonah

The men of Nineveh will rise up in the judgment with this generation and condemn it, for they repented at the preaching of Jonah; and indeed a greater than Jonah is here.   (Luke 11:32)

The Pharisees often demanded a sign from Jesus to prove his authority. Their scepticism and dry unbelief must have exasperated him. They had witnessed his many miracles but they seemed to want a personal one, on demand, to prove his case. He refused to play such games and to trivialise his divine power. Instead, Jesus warned that they would only have the sign of Jonah, a final sign to seal his authority. The prophet Jonah spent three days and nights in the belly of the great fish before being spewed out to safety. Jesus used this as an allegory of his death and resurrection to come. He was to be in the tomb for three days before he would be raised. The resurrection proved that he had been everything he had claimed to be.

"Today You Shall Be with Me in Paradise..."

Then one of the criminals who were hanged blasphemed Him, saying, "If You are the Christ, save Yourself and us."

> But the other, answering, rebuked him, saying, "Do you not even fear God, seeing you are under the same condemnation? And we indeed justly, for we receive the due reward of our deeds; but this Man has done nothing wrong." Then he said to Jesus, "Lord, remember me when You come into Your kingdom."
>
> And Jesus said to him, "Assuredly, I say to you, today you will be with Me in Paradise."   (Luke 23:39–43)

One of the criminals condemned with Jesus honoured him and implored him to remember him when the kingdom of God dawned. Jesus responded by assuring him that he would be with him that very day in paradise. Through the awful suffering on the cross, Jesus did not lose hope utterly that light would dawn beyond the darkness. "Paradise" is from a Persian word meaning a "pleasure garden" usually kept for the king. It is a metaphor for heaven elsewhere in the New Testament (e.g. 2 Corinthians 12:4). Some scholars speculate that this might have meant an in between state for many of the rabbis of the day, a joyful waiting room for heaven before the last judgment came. This is uncertain, but Jesus promised the repentant thief an afterlife, and that he would be where he was.

"In Three Days..."

> Now they were on the road, going up to Jerusalem, and Jesus was going before them; and they were amazed. And as they followed they were afraid. Then He took the twelve aside again and began to tell them the things that would happen to Him: "Behold, we are going up to Jerusalem, and the Son of Man will be betrayed to the chief priests and to the scribes; and they will condemn Him to death and deliver Him to the Gentiles; and they

will mock Him, and scourge Him, and spit on Him, and
kill Him. And the third day He will rise again."
(Mark 10:32–34)

Jesus predicted his own death and resurrection. He
warned the disciples that when they went to Jerusalem the
leaders would hand him over and he would be put to
death, but on the third day he would be raised up. They
were worried and shocked by this news. Jesus had
accepted, at a turning point in his ministry, that he was
going to be rejected and killed. We cannot imagine what it
must have been like to make that last journey to
Jerusalem, the holy city of the Jews, knowing what was
going to happen. By faith, he did so, obeying what he
believed was his Father's will. He would have to give his
life before the kingdom of God would come.

The reference to "on the third day" was more than historical or a literal prophecy, although it is those things. It
refers back to his teaching about "the sign of Jonah" and
other references in the Old Testament about deliverance
on the third day, such as Hosea 6:2:

After two days He will revive us;
On the third day He will raise us up.

Jesus was predicting that he would fulfil many Old
Testament hopes, and be "the sign of Jonah". He was a
greater teacher than Jonah (Luke 11:32) and just as Jonah
preached to the people of Nineveh and moved them to
repentance, so, too, the resurrection of Jesus can shake
our unbelief, calm our fears and assure us of the mercy
and eternal love of God.

It is to the resurrection of Jesus that we need to turn
next, to examine this in some detail.

5

The Resurrection

The story of the resurrection of Jesus fulfils the Old Testament hopes and lays the foundation for the whole of Christian faith and theology. If Jesus had not been raised, there would have been no church and no gospel message. The resurrection also gives all of us hope that there really is something after death and it opens a door for our spirits to be touched by God and renewed in this life.

The Four Gospels

Take hold of a Bible and read through the final chapters of the four Gospels if you have never ever done so. Look at Matthew 27:57 – 28:20; Mark 16; Luke 23:5 – 24:53 and John 19:38 – 21:25. This is not a great deal of reading, and familiarising yourself with the original story will help you through this chapter.

There are different slants on the same story in the Gospels, different details at times, some different characters and incidents recorded, but the same underlying episode. The women disciples, including Mary Magdalene, go to the tomb early on the Sunday morning after the Jewish Sabbath is over. They take spices to anoint and prepare the body according to Jewish custom, for there had not been sufficient time to do so on the Friday when all such labours had to cease as the Sabbath began. They go mourning and they get a shock. Mark's account is the barest, especially verses 1–8 in chapter 16. This is where scholars think the Gospel originally ended, an abrupt ending that leaves the reader reeling and wondering. Later scribes added a summary in verses 9–20 that sums up the resurrection accounts in the other Gospels. In the early ending of Mark, the women are amazed and rather scared, as is to be expected. They found the tomb open and empty and a vision of angels tells them that Jesus has risen. The type of tomb that had been used was a garden tomb, belonging to a rich man, Joseph of Arimathea. He had given this family tomb as a gift to the dead Master. Garden tombs were caves with chambers that were carved into the rock. A huge stone was rolled over the entrance to seal the tombs. This was to deter grave robbers who would go

looking for rich pickings in the valuables laid to rest with
the deceased, particularly in these tombs of the rich.

Yet the women found this tomb open and empty. A
Roman guard on the tomb had been overcome by the
supernatural power that opened it and fainted. All four
Gospels relate this incident in their own way, though it is
not really touched on in the other books of the New
Testament. There, the appearance of the risen Lord or the
bare fact of the resurrection is proclaimed.

The second ingredient of the resurrection stories is a
set of appearances of the risen Jesus. He appears to the
women, to Peter, to all the disciples assembled together, to
Thomas who doubted, to two people walking to the village
of Emmaus. Paul adds later that he appeared to 500 of the
brethren all at once – a story that he mentions only in
passing and we have no mention of it in the Gospels (c.f.
1 Corinthians 15:6). These appearances are fairly solid;
Jesus can be touched, he eats fish, he cooks breakfast for
the disciples and he breaks bread. He is also spiritual for
he can enter through locked doors and appear and disap-
pear at will. He is not always recognised; Mary Magdalene
thought he was the gardener until he spoke to her. The
people on the road to Emmaus did not know who he was
until he took bread and broke it. There is something
ambiguous and mysterious about the appearances. They
are not private visions for they are also tactile, and usually
affect several people at once. Even Paul's later vision of the
risen Lord whilst on the road to Damascus affected those
around him. He alone saw Jesus, but the men with him
heard something but saw nothing (see Acts 9).

Finally, there is the ingredient of renewed faith in the
resurrection story. The frightened disciples, hiding behind
locked doors in Jerusalem, or hiding away in Galilee

where some of them have returned to their fishing nets, were turned around and galvanised. They became rejoicing, praising, fearless witnesses and a number laid down their lives as martyrs. Something changed them.

These three ingredients of the empty tomb, the appearances and a renewed faith are the buzz and spiritual electricity behind the resurrection stories, a force that gave birth to Christianity as a new movement.

What Really Happened?

Sceptics try to explain away the story. Some theologians wonder if the empty-tomb story was a later legend, as it is not mentioned in the rest of the New Testament. They think something spiritual might have happened, but the body of Jesus was left to rot like anyone else's. Jesus might be alive in heaven and the disciples were renewed, but the body of Jesus was discarded and forgotten about. The problem with this is that all four Gospels tell the story as a bedrock, foundational narrative. If the tomb were not empty, it is hard to see why the Jews and Romans did not point this out, mocking the disciples for seeing things and following fables. There is no evidence of this and the nature of the tomb is passed over in silence in the ancient writers. If they knew it had been empty, that is not surprising.

If God really worked a stupendous miracle in the tomb, it is not hard to believe that the flesh and blood that he had taken in the incarnation was honoured and blessed. It was not forgotten or discarded but transformed. It was taken up into spirit. This is important, for Christian belief in a resurrected Jesus is not the same as belief in a resuscitated Jesus. The latter would have been what he was before, and he would have died again one day. Jesus is declared as risen not resuscitated in the Gospels. He was alive in a fabulously new way and could never die again.

The Body Was Stolen?

Some wonder if the disciples stole the body from the tomb and hid it, probably cremating it in the bonfires of the Valley of Hinnom outside Jerusalem to hide the evidence. This begs two questions. The first is how they got past the Roman guard assigned to the tomb. Matthew 27:62–66 states that Pilate ordered such a guard to be put in place. A Roman guard unit was made up of 16 men, usually. They would form a square formation around the object to be guarded. Four men would be on constant watch, one on each side. The other twelve would sleep with their heads facing in towards the object and the shift would change every four hours. Such a formation was trained to guard 36 yards against a battalion if necessary. They were no pushovers!

The other question is about the courage and the tenacity shown by the first Christians. Some of the apostles were prepared to die for their faith. You don't find conmen doing things like that. They would try to wriggle out of confrontation and save their skins. To all intents and purposes, the apostles really believed he was risen.

The Wrong Tomb?

Some wonder if the women went to the wrong tomb and made a mistake. Perhaps they found an empty tomb waiting for its owner to be interred. This is not really credible as the women were local and knew the terrain well. Also, a short walk (about fifteen minutes) from the centre of Jerusalem would have resolved the matter in the minds of the apostles. The Gospel accounts actually say that they went to check and they found the right tomb empty. A final nail in this particular coffin is that the testimony of women was not counted in Judaism at this time. It had no standing in law. Anything they reported would have to be checked out by the men.

Perhaps Jesus Did Not Die?

A more plausible explanation has sometimes been offered. This suggests that Jesus swooned, that he became comatose on the cross from all the pain and exertion (remember he had been whipped, also) and that people thought he was dead. He wasn't, and he revived later in the tomb. Maybe he had been drugged to kill the pain and the effects of this produced a paralysis that mimicked death. This was suggested in the controversial book *The Passover Plot* by Dr Hugh Schonfield in the 1960s, for example.

It is true that drugged wine was offered to the victims before they were nailed onto crosses. This was usually mixed with myrrh to deaden the senses and to prolong their exposure on a gibbet of public execution, and so the Romans encouraged it. The Gospels tell us that Jesus refused such offers, although just before he died a soldier offered him a sponge on a javelin that was soaked in such wine.

The normal type of drugged wine would not paralyse someone, though. One plant that could do this was the mandrake root. This was shredded, crushed and turned into a solution. If enough was taken it would produce

symptoms close to death with breathing being barely per-
ceptible. We have no evidence of this being used at the
crucifixion, although it is possible. However, there are
some difficulties with this theory.

It would have been extraordinarily difficult to gauge
the right dose, especially for a man undergoing the pain
and exertion of crucifixion. Too much would lead to death
as the system collapsed under the strain. Too little would
not paralyse.

Furthermore, John's account tells us that a soldier
plunged a lance into the side of Jesus to make sure that he
was dead. The description of blood and water pouring out
is anatomically correct when someone has died of crucifixion. The lungs fill with blood and fluid.

The overriding detail that scotches this rumour,
though, is the fact that the revived Jesus would look a
mess of blood and wounds. He would be extremely weak
and would not be able to convince anyone that he was
raised up and was the Lord of glory! A Jesus smuggled
away, quietly nursed and ending his days in some quiet
corner might be plausible but this would not account for
the burst of spiritual energy that came, the story of his rising, and the hope and dynamism it brought.

Hallucinations

Some wonder if the disciples and the women hallucinated.
It is known that the bereaved can see brief glimpses of
their loved ones. These are often mental tricks brought on
by grief. I recall the time when my grandmother died and
one of her daughters was convinced that she had caught a
fleeting glimpse of her in a crowd of shoppers. Grief does
strange things to us, that is true.

However, more substantial and revelatory encounters with the departed have been reported.

Another widely recorded phenomenon is when a person just knows that a friend or relative has died, even if they are miles away at the time. This might be a feeling – my wife went all cold at the moment when my father died. We only knew that he had been taken ill that morning, and did not realise how serious it was. We were phoned later that day with the sad news.

Some might see an apparition in their room, where the deceased person assures them that they are all right. This happened with the poet Wilfred Owen. During the First World War, Harold Owen was on active duty in the navy. In his cabin, one day, he saw Wilfred sitting in a chair. He felt overcome, could hardly move, and watched Wilfred smile a most gentle smile, and then he was gone.

Another moving case involved a dying old woman seeing deceased family members coming to collect her. She was confused to see one with a baby, but then it dawned that it was her granddaughter's baby. The fact is that she did not know that the child had just died, many miles away. Her son had kept the news from her in her dying hours.

More common is a dream encounter with the deceased, such as that of Lord Jenkins, who dreamed of Anthony Crosland, an old friend. Jenkins was on business in Rome, and Crosland was dying in Oxford. Crosland told him that he was "perfectly all right" even though he was about to die. Jenkins woke up and was phoned with the news that his friend had just died.

These might be genuine perceptions of the departed, but they are oral, audible, and not tactile in any way. The resurrection appearances are audible *and* tactile. They are yet more substantial and of a different order from these common experiences. Whatever they were, they were far more than mere hallucinations and more profound than dream visitations.

The Disciples Felt Guilty

Another suggestion is that the first disciples felt guilty for abandoning their Master when he was arrested, particularly Peter, who denied him publicly three times. This might have propelled them into martyrdom out of a profound sense of remorse and a penitential motive. This could have happened in such circumstances, though it does not fit the facts of the larger picture we have. The belief in the resurrection renewed faith and brought great joy. It was a spiritual, living affair and not some driven, psychotic, anxious business. Guilty people do not produce a living faith in others.

Can We Trust the Gospels?

Some wonder if the Gospel accounts are so much later than the events they purport to describe that they are legendary and untrustworthy. Perhaps Jesus really stayed dead but his message lived on in his disciples and much, much later there were tales and legends about people seeing him again and the tomb being found empty. It is true that the Gospels were written fairly late in the first century, but they were based on years of oral tradition and other written accounts that circulated among the first Christians. In that day and age, things were not always written down for some time because people remembered things more easily than we do now. Theirs was a culture that passed things down by word of mouth much more than we do. Also, there are numerous New Testament documents that predate the Gospels. Some of Paul's letters such as Romans, the Corinthian correspondence, Galatians and the letters to the Thessalonians take us into the 40s and 50s AD. There is a clear belief in the resurrection contained in these, and in all of the documents of the New Testament. In 1 Corinthians 15 Paul defends the belief in the resurrection against certain sceptics. He argues that without it their faith is in vain and he expounds the doctrine in a mature and considered way. He teaches that the resurrection body is a spiritual body and not a resuscitated body of flesh and blood:

> The body is sown in corruption; it is raised in incorruption. It is sown in dishonor; it is raised in glory.
>
> (1 Corinthians 15:42–43)

Also, in the early chapters of the Acts of the Apostles there are traces of some very primitive Christian material in the passages describing the early preaching of Peter. There are concepts and words that are simplistic and undeveloped when compared with later Christian thinking. Many scholars thus recognise that there is very early material preserved here. Yet, in these very early traditions, Jesus is proclaimed as risen. There is no evidence of the disciples simply carrying on the teaching of their Master; they proclaimed him as the risen Lord instead.

The resurrection has been called the foundation of New Testament theology for this reason.

> And if Christ is not risen, then our preaching is empty and your faith is also empty.
>
> (1 Corinthians 15:14)

Various New Testament scholars, who might not all be believers, admit that the evidence suggests that the first disciples did believe that they had resurrection appearances and experiences of Jesus. They are not prepared to say any more than this as disinterested scholars, but the veracity of the experiences is undeniable.

> The disciples' conviction that they had seen the risen Christ, their permanent relocation to Jerusalem, their principled inclusion of gentiles as gentiles – all these are historical bedrock, facts known past doubting about the earliest community after Jesus' death…
> (Paula Fredriksen, *Jesus of Nazareth, King of the Jews*)

> That Jesus' followers… had resurrection experiences is, in my judgement, a fact. What the reality was that gave rise to the experiences I do not know… we know that after his death his followers experienced what they described as the "resurrection": the appearance of a living but transformed person who had actually died. They believed this, they lived it, and they died for it. In the process they created a movement, a movement that in many ways went far beyond Jesus' message. Their movement grew and grew… (E.P. Sanders, *The Historical Figure of Jesus*)

Sanders also points out the untidy nature of the different Gospel accounts with their different details and small contradictions. Having the women as the first witnesses would have been intellectual suicide unless it had actually happened. If the disciples had sat down to invent a cock-and-bull story, then they went about it disastrously. As Sanders points out: "Moreover, a calculated deception should have produced more unanimity. Instead there seem to have been competitors: 'I saw him first!' 'No, I did!'… "

The Gospel accounts smack too much of reality and the untidy nature of life. They speak of being surprised by something they had never expected and they were sometimes lost for words to know how to describe it.

Far from the death of Jesus being the end of his mission, a revival of faith broke out. Sanders notes: "That is, they did not give up his idea that the kingdom would come; they now expected him to return from heaven to establish it."

The lawyer Frank Morrison searched through the evidence of the Gospel accounts in his book *Who Moved the Stone?* He began as a sceptic but he concluded as a believer: "There may be, and as the writer thinks, there certainly is, a deep and profoundly historical basis for that much disputed sentence in the Apostles' Creed – 'The *third day* he rose again from the dead.'... "

Just Like Elvis?

Richard Dawkins, the celebrated atheist, in an interview with a Christian magazine, has scoffed that no scholars take the contradictory stories seriously, and that belief in the risen Jesus is like saying that you have seen Elvis. It is all imagination and make-believe, pure fable.

This is a total exaggeration. The differences are not so great, the common features are crystal clear, and something did happen, something objective that turned this group around. Serious scholars do recognise this, as shown above. Elvis fans can be oddballs, who see Elvis at odd times in odd places, with no rhyme or reason. Their lives are not changed, they are not spiritually refreshed, and they have no new moral courage. However, that is what happened to the first disciples, and there's the difference. Something changed them, something that cannot be shaken out of the historical record no matter how hard we try. The scholar F.F. Bruce once called this an irreducible "X" factor.

Some might not want to face up to this – to the fact that all rational accounts of the resurrection fall flat on their faces and still leave us with a huge puzzle. They don't want to face it because it is so challenging. It might just mean that God is out there and Jesus wants to do business with us.

A Piece of Cloth?

The Shroud of Turin is a long, ancient piece of cloth that bears the markings of a human figure, a man who has been scourged by a Roman whip and crucified. The anatomical details are accurate, more accurate than the many medieval paintings of the cross that exist. It is claimed to be the actual burial shroud that was wrapped around the body of Jesus and placed in the tomb (c.f. John 19:40). This cloth was photographed for the first time in 1898 by the Italian Secondo Pia. To his amazement he found that the negative plates showed a positive image. The features of the crucified man were even clearer! That meant that a negative image was on the cloth.

The late twentieth century saw many scientific examinations and microscopic examination of the image. The image lies on the surface of the fibres and seems to be some form of degradation of the actual fibre and not a pigment or a burn. There are traces of blood and also of many pollen samples that come only from the Holy Land. No one can work out how this image could have been formed. Many attempts have been made to reproduce it but all have failed.

Carbon dating in the 1990s suggested that it was a medieval forgery, and it must be noted that its first definite, recorded appearance was in the fourteenth century in France. However, later studies have revealed a coating over the surface of the cloth that has formed over the years, a bio-plastic layer that ancient objects can produce. It is argued that this would have affected the carbon dating and some are attempting to have the cloth retested.

Historians have also made out an impressive case that might trace the whereabouts of the cloth back before the fourteenth century. The first recorded owner was a descendant of a Crusader knight who might have acquired it from Constantinople, where a famed image of Christ was kept, supposedly not made by human hands. This can be traced back to ancient Syria and it has its own legends about how it came from Judea. Maybe, possibly. We cannot close our minds to this old relic. But what of the resurrection?

One theory of how the image was formed was that it was a split-second flash of energy that occurred as the resurrection took place. This has been compared with the release of nuclear energy in the atomic bomb at Hiroshima, when people directly below it were carbonised and a shadow was permanently left on buildings. The energy of the resurrection was of a different order, of course, a spiritual energy that we cannot understand. Fascinating, and maybe true; it is a speculation that might back up belief in the resurrection, but that belief does not depend upon its veracity.

A Mystery

We can rightly argue that the resurrection is based upon fact, but it is a wonderful mystery. It was something transcendent, spiritual and ineffable. The Eastern churches paint beautiful icons of Jesus, the saints and scenes from the Bible stories. I recall visiting Delphi in Greece and seeing these for the first time, in any great number, in a small Orthodox church there. They took my breath away as I walked around and looked all the way up the walls and around the domed roof. I am a very visual person, responding to images, and a great lover of comic-strip art. Icons might be sacred and more revered, but they appealed to someone of my tastes. When you examine the icons of the resurrection, two different types are found. The first is of the myrrh-bearing women approaching the empty tomb where an angel sits. The second is of the risen Lord in Hades/Sheol, reaching down and grabbing Adam's wrist as he starts to rise up, taking the Old Testament saints with him as the grave is opened.

Striking images, but they do not try to depict the moment of resurrection. That is a mystery not for human eyes.

C.S. Lewis writes, intriguingly, that the risen body of Jesus could pass through solid doors because it was more solid, not less, than they. To Jesus, this world is ghostly, for he is alive with resurrection life, the existence of heaven. Heaven is far more real, far more solid than our existence. Interesting thoughts that underline the deep mystery of the resurrection. It is something other-worldly and heavenly bursting into this realm. Hence our exasperation as well as our joy.

Speculations and Theologians

There are some intriguing and inspiring speculations, made by theologians, from time to time. Take the Catholic priest Teilhard de Chardin, for example, early in the twentieth century. He was also a scientist interested in palaeontology and early human development. He speculated that the process of creation was destined to move forward to a final consummation that he called "the Omega Point". He was a firm believer in the theory of evolution, something that different Christians have divergent opinions about, but he saw this as theistic, under the hand of God. The world was going somewhere and was not just a story full of sound and fury, signifying nothing. He identified the resurrection with the Omega Point. The risen body of Jesus shone with the life of the end of all things, the divine consummation and joy. It was the light at the end of the tunnel, a pledge of future glory and all things would one day be conformed to it.

The German theologian Jürgen Moltmann has written much about hope. He was a conscript in the German army in World War Two and he has reflected on the terrible suffering that humanity can experience. He sees the resurrection as a pledge of future glory, too; as a sign that hope will win out, that light will shine in the darkness. It is a beacon and an anchor through the storms of life.

These two theologians echo Paul in Colossians 1:18 where he describes the risen Jesus as "the firstborn from the dead".

There is a link with the cosmos and the risen Lord, for if his flesh was transfigured and raised up, so too can all matter be one day until the whole earth is filled with the knowledge of the Lord as the waters cover the sea (Isaiah 11:9).

Resurrection is...

The resurrection of Jesus has been compared to a comet. The ball of hard matter at the nose is the historical event that emptied the tomb. The blaze of fire that swept from this ignited the faith of the first Christians. The long tail reaches out to us today and touches lives still. The event 2,000 years ago set something in motion, a spiritual energy that can strike people today. The effect of the resurrection gives new, spiritual life now as well as beyond the grave. The New Testament writings are full of this sense of inner illumination and redirection:

> But if the Spirit of Him who raised Jesus from the dead dwells in you, He who raised Christ from the dead will also give life to your mortal bodies through His Spirit who dwells in you. (Romans 8:11)

If we leave aside all the historical investigations and evidence, the best, most abiding evidence of the resurrection can be found in changed lives and renewed faith today. The person who turns to Christ and finds a new start, a hope that was not there before, and a walk of faith that did not exist prior to their conversion, is a living witness to the resurrection of Jesus, the greatest and most hopeful mystery ever.

A Place of Safety

> Then, the same day at evening, being the first day of the week, when the doors were shut where the disciples were assembled, for fear of the Jews, Jesus came and stood in the midst, and said to them, "Peace be with you." When He had said this, He showed them His hands and His

side. Then the disciples were glad when they saw the Lord.

So Jesus said to them again, "Peace to you! As the Father has sent Me, I also send you." And when He had said this, He breathed on them, and said to them, "Receive the Holy Spirit. If you forgive the sins of any, they are forgiven them; if you retain the sins of any, they are retained."

Now Thomas, called the Twin, one of the twelve, was not with them when Jesus came. The other disciples therefore said to him, "We have seen the Lord." So he said to them, "Unless I see in His hands the print of the nails, and put my finger into the print of the nails, and put my hand into His side, I will not believe."

And after eight days His disciples were again inside, and Thomas with them. Jesus came, the doors being shut, and stood in the midst, and said, "Peace to you!" Then He said to Thomas, "Reach your finger here, and look at My hands; and reach your hand here, and put it into My side. Do not be unbelieving, but believing."

And Thomas answered and said to Him, "My Lord and my God!"

Jesus said to him, "Thomas, because you have seen Me, you have believed. Blessed are those who have not seen and yet have believed." (John 20:19–29)

Thomas doubted that the Lord had risen; he was invited to touch and see for himself. Jesus, though risen in a glorified body, had retained the scars from the cross. Thomas was invited to touch the wounds in the Master's hands and to place his hand in his side. People wonder why those wounds were still there if everything in the resurrection is supposed to be perfect. Jesus chose to carry the wounds for all eternity when they could have been wiped away in shining light. He carries the marks on his body in heaven that all ages will witness the great sacrifice and the love he has for his creation. As Charles Wesley put it:

> The dear tokens of his Passion
> Still His dazzling body bears…
> ("Lo, He comes with clouds descending", 1758.)

Thomas was blessed, but even more blessed are those who come to believe later. They will believe without touching and seeing:

> Blessed are those who have not seen and yet have believed.
> (John 20:29b)

This is addressed to all of us in the generations that followed those first disciples. There are occasional reports of visions of the risen Jesus, often in dream like states, but sometimes in waking life. I once had such an experience, in the middle of the night, in a dream that did not feel like dreaming. It felt too real, as though a veil had parted and I stood in another dimension. The Lord spoke with me about certain matters soon after I had come to believe in him as a young man. Such encounters are very real but rare, and most find faith through the testimony of the Scriptures, the witness of believing Christians and the power of the Holy Spirit. Take courage from Jesus' words to Thomas: "Blessed are those who have not seen and yet have believed."

Another great truth in the Thomas story is the invitation to place his hand in the side of Christ. Christian writers through the ages have seen a rich and beautiful symbol in this, of coming into a place of blessing and safety by giving our lives to Christ. Devotional writers look to passages in the Psalms about God blessing us with honey from clefts in the rocks, or how God is a place of safety and a sure refuge (c.f. Psalm 81:16 and Psalm 46:1). They made a mystical, symbolic link with the side of Christ as such a cleft in a rock. We can find peace and refuge there, too.

> They pierced His hands and feet, and opened His side with a lance, and through these clefts I may "suck honey out of the rock and oil out of the flinty rock", which is to "taste and see that the Lord is good"... Where, more clearly than in your wounds, does it shine out that you, Lord, are meek and humble and abounding in mercy?
>
> (*St Bernard of Clairvaux*)

> I am He who lives, and was dead, and behold, I am alive forevermore. Amen. And I have the keys of Hades and of Death... (Revelation 1:18)

6

Judgment

Jesus sometimes warned people of a judgment to come after death. They would be called before their Creator to give an account of themselves. They would face God in all his awesome holiness. How would they be, then? Would they be ready, full of regrets, welcomed or rejected? He calls us to safety, to trust him and to be covered by his forgiveness.

Warnings

We don't like to think about difficult and unpleasant matters. Warnings about judgment are, perhaps, parts of the Bible that we would rather ignore or skim over. But they are there, and should be taken seriously. Some form of divine judgment is to be a reality.

In one parable, Jesus tells people not to care too much about their wealth and to worry more about the state of their souls. He describes a foolish man who built bigger barns to store more and more crops, looking forward to what he would spend his wealth on. Then, that night, he died. A person is a fool who gathers earthly wealth but does not have a rich relationship with God.

> Then one from the crowd said to Him, "Teacher, tell my brother to divide the inheritance with me."
>
> But He said to him, "Man, who made Me a judge or an arbitrator over you?" And He said to them, "Take heed and beware of covetousness, for one's life does not consist in the abundance of the things he possesses."
>
> Then He spoke a parable to them, saying: "The ground of a certain rich man yielded plentifully. And he thought within himself, saying, 'What shall I do, since I have no room to store my crops?' So he said, 'I will do this: I will pull down my barns and build greater, and there I will store all my crops and my goods. And I will say to my soul, "Soul, you have many goods laid up for many years; take your ease; eat, drink, and be merry." ' But God said to him, 'Fool! This night your soul will be required of you; then whose will those things be which you have provided?'
>
> "So is he who lays up treasure for himself, and is not rich toward God."   (Luke 12:13–21)

In the parable of the Sheep and the Goats, Jesus said that some would be blessed at the Judgment and brought into God's presence; others would be sent away. He warns about the possibility of "eternal punishment".

> Then the King will say to those on His right hand, "Come, you blessed of My Father, inherit the kingdom prepared for you from the foundation of the world: for I was hungry and you gave Me food; I was thirsty and you gave Me drink; I was a stranger and you took Me in; I was naked and you clothed Me; I was sick and you visited Me; I was in prison and you came to Me."...
>
> Then He will also say to those on the left hand, "Depart from Me, you cursed, into the everlasting fire prepared for the devil and his angels: for I was hungry and you gave Me no food; I was thirsty and you gave Me no drink; I was a stranger and you did not take Me in, naked and you did not clothe Me, sick and in prison and you did not visit Me."   (Matthew 25:34–36, 41–43)

Hell?

Jesus said some hard and unpleasant things about eternal punishment and the subject of Hell. "Hell" is a translation of the Hebrew "Gehenna". "Gehenna" was the Hebrew term for the Valley of Hinnom outside Jerusalem. This was the rubbish tip where rubbish was burnt in a constant fire. Jesus uses it as a symbol of the fire of God's judgment on sin in our lives. He uses vivid and shocking imagery about this, warning that, for some, there is the terrible possibility that they will use their divinely given gift of free will to reject God – for ever!

And if your eye causes you to sin, pluck it out. It is better
for you to enter the kingdom of God with one eye, rather
than having two eyes, to be cast into hell fire –
(Mark 9:47)

In another saying, Jesus warns people not to fear the death
of the body, but those who can kill the soul by corrupting
it with evil. Hell is their fate.

And do not fear those who kill the body but cannot kill the
soul. But rather fear Him who is able to destroy both soul
and body in hell.   (Matthew 10:28)

These are worrying statements, and there are different
interpretations made by Christians of what is actually
meant by "hell". It seems bizarre and unjust for God to
build an everlasting torture chamber and allow it to exist
in his universe. It sounds downright cruel and sadistic.

Jesus uses symbols. We are not dealing with actual fire
but with a state of alienation and separation from God,
from all that is love, light and life. That is a dreadful state
to be in. We are dealing with the terrible possibility that
some will reject the love of God, no matter what. They will
be destroyed by their own evil, and refuse all help. Hell is
thus a state of being eternally separated from God. Some
speculate that, in choosing this anti-life stance, it means
that a damned soul simply evaporates and ceases to exist.
This is the "annihilation theory" of eternal punishment.
Others feel that the Scriptures suggest that the damned
live on, but lost and unable to turn to the light. To continue to exist without hope of God is eternal punishment.
Where this is and what happens there is beyond our

knowledge. The Book of Revelation speaks in this way about those who are not found in the Book of Life:

> And anyone not found written in the Book of Life was cast into the lake of fire.   (Revelation 20:15)

C.S. Lewis has some imaginative speculations about this in *The Great Divorce*. There, the damned are like grey ghosts who move further and further away from others, moving out into the mists until they are forgotten and unheard of again. He hints that they fade away, little by little, as they move further and further away from the possibility of redemption. This is just his idea, though. He is claiming no special visions or revelations.

Putting Ourselves in Hell?

Can a good God really send some people into a state of eternal separation? It can be argued that, as he is holy and righteous, sinners cannot stand to be in his presence; they recoil, back away, flee his light. Righteousness demands that they depart from his presence, and they do, internally driven to embrace the darkness.

It is perhaps more that some put *themselves* into hell. The modern *Catechism of the Catholic Church*, for example, states: "This state of definitive *self-exclusion* from communion with God and the blessed is called 'hell.'..." (italics mine)

This follows the statement in John 3:19–20 that some run away from the light for all they are worth!

> And this is the condemnation, that the light has come into the world, and men loved darkness rather than light,

because their deeds were evil. For everyone practicing evil hates the light and does not come to the light, lest his deeds should be exposed.   (John 3:19–20)

Yet there are the judgments issued in parables such as that of the Sheep and the Goats, where some are declared to be damned by God. Perhaps it is the same thing from twin angles: a hardened, unrepentant heart flees the Light; the Light recoils from the sinner and sends them away.

Referring back to Near Death Experiences (NDEs) that people relate, there are few actual examples of a place or sense of judgment. A handful of people have been frightened, but more common is a more gentle sense of being judged akin to standing in the presence of the Light. Remember the case of George Ritchie, who recognised the figure of Jesus as the Being of Light who stood before him. He felt that Jesus saw right through him, to his innermost secrets of the heart, and yet he was loved through and through. He felt as though he were not worthy and wanted to bow down in worship.

Another case, this time not that of a consciously Christian believer, tells of a sense of being placed in the shoes of everyone whom he had hurt as a life review flashed by: "I remember one particular incident in this review when, as a child, I yanked my little sister's Easter basket away from her, because there was a toy in it that I wanted. Yet, in the review, I felt her feelings of disappointment and losses and rejection. I was the very people I hurt and I was the very people that I helped to feel good."

We must not, of course, place such stories on a par with the Scriptures. We do not know how real or genuine these NDEs are, after all, but this sort of material is certainly interesting.

What about those who have never heard?

What about those who have never had a chance to hear the gospel? This would apply to someone from a nation where another faith is practised, or a person who has never personally understood what Jesus meant, even if they have heard of him. What about the honest, devout adherents of other faiths, also?

A second chance sounds like a reasonable request, but what might such a chance be like? And is there any suggestion of this in the New Testament?

C.S. Lewis speculated that the dead might be given a second chance to respond (after death) in his story *The Great Divorce*. Here, a busload of a dozen souls is taken from the grim, grey outskirts of hell to lush plains on the outskirts of heaven. Saints and angels come across to invite them in. All but one, incredibly, refuse. They make their excuses and return. Their sins have gone too deep, their souls are twisted and corrupted. The one repentant soul has to encounter by holy fire and it hurts. Yet, through this pain, there comes new life. Hell is then imagined as a grey, miserable place where these souls cannot stand other company. They drift off into the mists, as mentioned earlier, forgotten and lost. But this is just his imagination, his opinion.

Is there a second chance after death? Many Christians would shout: "NO!" This strongly negative response is because to speak of such a thing might water down the gospel or give false hope and comfort. People will sit back, ignore the call of God, and think "Oh, well, it'll be all right in the end!" This need not be the case, of course, and Lewis showed how impossible it would be for many unredeemed souls even if a second chance were offered. His maxim might be summed up as "Turn to God, the sooner the better, or it may be never!" We cannot say what will happen to those who have not heard about Jesus (and not just those in foreign places, but people in "Christian" countries who do not really understand who Jesus is). People who have never really heard have not had a *first* chance! We are not allowed to be their judge. God alone is that, and, as he says to Abraham, "Shall not the Judge of all the earth do right?" (Genesis 18:25).

The apostle Paul states that any who have not heard about God's revelation in the Scriptures will be judged by the light of their conscience.

> for when Gentiles, who do not have the law, by nature do the things in the law, these, although not having the law, are a law to themselves, who show the work of the law written in their hearts, their conscience also bearing witness, and between themselves their thoughts accusing or else excusing them) in the day when God will judge the secrets of men by Jesus Christ, according to my gospel.
>
> (Romans 2:14–16)

One of the other letters suggests that Jesus preached to the spirits of the dead in between his death and resurrection.

> For Christ also suffered once for sins, the just for the unjust, that He might bring us to God, being put to death in the flesh but made alive by the Spirit, by whom also He went and preached to the spirits in prison...
>
> For this reason the gospel was preached also to those who are dead, that they might be judged according to men in the flesh, but live according to God in the spirit.
>
> (1 Peter 3:18–19; 4:6)

These references are notoriously difficult to interpret. Was this preaching *just* to those who had died before Jesus came? Medieval mystery plays included a dramatisation of this event, called *The Harrowing of Hell*. It must have been noisy and great fun for the actors, playing devils who banged pots and pans and rattled spears as Jesus walked out of a dragon's mouth, free. Satan was defeated and the risen Lord led the heroes of the Old Testament to freedom with him. They had been waiting for his day.

The Eastern churches have an icon of this event, showing the risen Jesus pulling Adam by the wrist out of the grave. In Jesus, the second Adam, all are made alive.

So, the Scriptures might apply only to the saints of the Old Testament whom Jesus called out of Sheol (in Hebrew) or Hades (in Greek), the waiting room for the Judgment. Others wonder if there are deeper and more eternal possibilities in these passages. Was the preaching at a specific place and time, or does time have any bearing in the afterlife? If time ceases to exist as we know it beyond this physical universe, then the preaching might be an eternal event. This brings us back to the ideas in *The Great Divorce*.

Here, we deal with mysteries and we cannot be anyone else's judge. We are responsible for our own lives. The New Testament writers warn of coming judgment, and urge people to turn to Jesus, to accept mercy and peace won by his sacrifice on the cross. There is the terrible possibility of being separated from God, separated by our own sins for ever. They do not make personal judgments upon anyone's actual and personal eternal destiny, though. Nowhere in Scripture are we allowed to do that. But there are warnings that should be listened to. Look at the first preaching on the Day of Pentecost, for example:

> Then Peter said to them, "Repent, and let every one of you be baptized in the name of Jesus Christ for the remission of sins; and you shall receive the gift of the Holy Spirit. For the promise is to you and to your children, and to all who are afar off, as many as the Lord our God will call."
>
> (Acts 2:38–39)

We can be sure of our salvation and our acceptance by God. Let us preach that from the rooftops and bring light to many. What we cannot do, what we have no scriptural warrant to do, is to judge anyone's eternal destiny who has not heard of salvation through Jesus. That is off limits. That is for God alone to judge. We warn, we urge, we extend hope, but we cannot close the door on anyone. We do not know their hearts, and neither do we know what might happen as they go through life, or even what might happen within the souls of some people as they approach death. This can be holy ground as defences are finally lowered and they might hear God for the first time. As the saintly Curé d'Ars, Jean Marie Vianney said in the nineteenth century: "The mercy of God is faster than the flight of the eagle." Perhaps what some call a "second chance" is this hearing, this revelation of Jesus in all his glory as people go through the process of crossing over. We do not know quite where this starts and finishes. Let us be open-minded.

Many are the stories of such conversions which I have heard of in pastoral ministry. Many are inarticulate, with a sense of profound peace coming over the dying person and then they let go and pass on. We do not know what is happening within them.

I have prayed at the bedside of many of the dying. Some are unconscious and I have prayed the light of

Christ over them and pleaded the precious blood for them. Sometimes there is a stirring and an inarticulate murmuring as I do this. They calm down and a sense of God's presence is there. What has transpired? What transaction has been made in their hearts? I do not know; I am not allowed to judge.

I heard the moving story of one widow who had been born again and moved in the early days of charismatic renewal. Her husband, who was older than her, was very resistant and veered between agnosticism and atheism. He was prayed for time and time again, and nothing changed. He was diagnosed with cancer and his wife placed a prayer cloth, anointed with holy oil, under his pillow. As he drifted into unconsciousness, she prayed beside him and read the Scriptures. Just before he died, there was a peace, and a reaching out to touch her hand. She really felt that he had met Jesus, and had made his peace. He could speak no words, though.

I was speaking to a minister recently who knows an evangelist, John Wessells, who feels called to preach and worship in wards where people lie in a coma. He senses that God is ministering to them in ways that we do not comprehend. He has known of some who recover and have been converted whilst in the coma! God met them in their spirits and in their dreams.

We must not judge; we are not allowed to condemn.

Purgatory?

Roman Catholics believe in a state called purgatory. This is in between heaven and hell.

There is much misunderstanding about this. It is for people who are saved, who are Christ's. It is not just a grey zone for people who are not very good but not very bad, as is popularly assumed. The idea is that we are purified, cleansed, purged of sin and healed up so that we can step into the full, dazzling presence of God after we have believed and partaken of grace in this life. Thus, Catholics speak of the "holy souls" in purgatory. The belief has gone through various forms and expressions and was only defined as Catholic doctrine as late as 1439 at the Council of Florence.

It began as a series of speculations by early Church Fathers such as Tertullian in the early third century AD, Augustine of Hippo in the fifth century AD and Pope Gregory the Great in the sixth century AD. In their works, it was assumed that God would need to cleanse us after death to be ready for heaven. Augustine referred to scriptures such as 1 Corinthians 3:10–15, where the fire of God will test our lives and our works, even if we are among the "saved".

In the Renaissance period, the idea of purgatory was painful but joyful at one and the same time. In Dante's *Divine Comedy*, the redeemed souls in purgatory rejoice together as they advance up a mountain towards the joy of heaven. It was a community endeavour.

By the late Middle Ages and the Reformation period, purgatory had become a lesser hell. The whole system of indulgences had come into play. These were given for pious acts and they promised release from time in purgatory. The prayers and good works of the living had been thought to benefit the souls in purgatory for some time (even Augustine had held that) but this was a much more streamlined system with its own salesmen. Luther's protest in 1517 was primarily against the sales tactics and the traffic in questionable relics. Even he believed in purgatory at that time, though he rejected it later.

In later times, the emphasis in the Catholic Church has been more individual though joyful. Cardinal Newman's *The Dream of Gerontius* charts the progress of a soul being taken to heaven by the angels. As it approaches Jesus it bows low and recoils, sinking lower and lower into the cleansing fires of purgatory until it is ready to embrace him:

> There I will sing my absent Lord and Love;
> Take me away,
> That sooner I may rise and go above,
> And seek Him in the truth of everlasting day.

In more recent Catholic theology and practice, purgatory is affirmed but lies rather in the background. The Catholic Church went through sweeping changes and a huge "makeover" in the Second Vatican Council in the 1960s. It could be said that the Bible is more central in its life and worship than it has been for a long time, although, of course, for many Protestants, these reforms did not go far enough.

Purgatory, then, is not in the Bible as such. There are ideas about being tested by fire, as mentioned above, in 1 Corinthians. There is also the idea that we shall be like Christ one day (1 John 3:2) and we shall see him as he is. In the Old Testament, Malachi 3:1–3 and 4:1–3 speak of a purifying fire brought by the Lord. This begins as we turn to him and start a process of growth in holiness, but there is a culmination, a completion, as we stand before Jesus after death. As Paul says, "He who has begun a good work in you will complete it until the day of Jesus Christ" (Philippians 1:6). Hans Küng is a Catholic theologian who is rather suspect as far as the Vatican is concerned, but he has a definition of purgatory that could be an ecumenical success. He argues that purgatory should be understood only as a moment, a healing and sanctifying encounter with the love of God as we cross over to his presence. Time as we know it does not exist in the Beyond. Might all Christians be able to agree that there is a purifying, sifting, cleansing, healing encounter with God as we cross over and enter heaven? Might this be what it means to have our works tested as if by fire, to see Christ and be like him, and to have the good work finished within us? The term "purgatory" is too loaded and controversial, but this idea of blazing, purifying encounter that completes the work of salvation within us might be fruitful ground for ecumenical dialogue. It is the prolonged process with the mechanical means of dispensation by the prayers and almsgiving of the living that is rejected. This is discarded as it is not scriptural and it is feared that it denies the work of the cross. Salvation is by grace from start to finish. Though prayers offered are acts of charity in the Roman Catholic mind, that can only be a good thing for the departed.

Also, the early speculations about purgatory were held only in the Western church. The Eastern Orthodox Churches never taught a doctrine of purgatory as the West did, and do not do so today. It is rejected as unapostolic.

Prayer for the Dead?

Another point of disagreement between churches is the practice of prayer for the dead. Much of this is closely bound up with a belief in purgatory, as outlined above. Not all of it needs to be, though.

Some form of prayer mentioning the departed dates

back to very early in the history of the church. It is not biblical, but it *is* very early. For example, there are prayer inscriptions on Christian tombs from the first century AD, some dating from as early as 40–50 AD. To quote just two of these, one has the petition "Jesus, help" and the other "Jesus, let him rise". Were these prayers actually intended to change the destiny of the departed soul, or were they merely comforting affirmations of what the mourners believed Jesus was going to do for their departed brother or sister?

Prayers for the departed continued in one form or another right up to the Reformation. The Reformers rejected such prayers along with their rejection of purgatory and the whole medieval apparatus of praying and offering for the souls there.

The Eastern churches have prayer for the departed but this is mainly a series of petitions for their peaceful repose to comfort the mourners. A recent Orthodox description of such a book of prayers, for example, says that they are "prayed as an act of love for the departed, whilst also being an effective spiritual therapy for those who remain". To quote one such prayer:

> In the place of Thy rest, O Lord, where all Thy Saints repose, give rest also to the soul of Thy servant; for Thou lovest mankind.

There is also a tradition of praying for the souls of the departed who are awaiting the Judgment. The Orthodox churches teach that there is a world of the dead, Hades, where the souls await the Day of Judgment. Jesus preached there and led many out to freedom when he rose again. The Orthodox believe that our prayers might aid people there now to repent and seek Christ. One Orthodox saint believed that he had freed the soul of the Roman emperor Trajan, for whom he had a burden in prayer. After the Last Judgment, though, a person's eternal destiny is fixed and prayers will then avail nothing for the lost.

As Bishop Kallistos (Timothy) Ware put it:

> It is heretical to say that all must be saved, for this is to deny free will; but it is legitimate to hope that all may be saved. Until the Last Day comes, we must not despair of another's salvation, but must long and pray for the reconciliation of all without exception. No one must be excluded from our loving intercession.
>
> (*The Orthodox Church*, p. 262)

Fascinating, daring and original, but not actually biblical. It is extra-biblical tradition and speculation which Reformed Christians are wary of. A waiting room for the Judgment, where souls might repent, seems to contradict the story of the Rich Man and Lazarus, too.

> There was a certain rich man who was clothed in purple and fine linen and fared sumptuously every day. But there was a certain beggar named Lazarus, full of sores, who was laid at his gate, desiring to be fed with the crumbs which fell from the rich man's table. Moreover the dogs came and licked his sores. So it was that the beggar died, and was carried by the angels to Abraham's bosom. The rich man also died and was buried. And being in torments in Hades, he lifted up his eyes and saw Abraham afar off, and Lazarus in his bosom.
>
> Then he cried and said, "Father Abraham, have mercy on me, and send Lazarus that he may dip the tip of his finger in water and cool my tongue; for I am tormented in

this flame." But Abraham said, "Son, remember that in your lifetime you received your good things, and likewise Lazarus evil things; but now he is comforted and you are tormented. And besides all this, between us and you there is a great gulf fixed, so that those who want to pass from here to you cannot, nor can those from there pass to us."

Then he said, "I beg you therefore, father, that you would send him to my father's house, for I have five brothers, that he may testify to them, lest they also come to this place of torment." Abraham said to him, "They have Moses and the prophets; let them hear them." And he said, "No, father Abraham; but if one goes to them from the dead, they will repent." But he said to him, "If they do not hear Moses and the prophets, neither will they be persuaded though one rise from the dead."

(Luke 16:19–31)

Jesus indicates that an impenetrable gulf separates those destined for heaven and those for damnation. Whether this describes a general state or just a particular case of one individual is a moot point, but many believers would be very wary of feeling that the souls of the departed are able to move towards God if they end up in this place unredeemed. Again, we handle profound mysteries and we must be very, very careful with our speculations.

The vexed philosophical question of the relevance of time in the afterlife comes to the fore again. How can there be a "waiting" period in eternity? We handle mysteries. Some, such as the Orthodox, would say that our prayers within *this* time frame are all present to God simultaneously and they might have an impact that we do not understand in the grand scheme of things. All of reality – of earth and eternity – is present to God as "now". How "time" works beyond the space/time continuum, in whatever stretched form, is outside our knowledge and we play with paradoxes and spin on pinheads with the angels.

The Anglican Communion often dubs itself a "bridge church" between Catholic and Protestant. Anglicans have developed a form of prayer for the departed which is meant to be no more than a memorial, "an act of love for the departed and a spiritual therapy for those who remain". In the *Common Worship* book of the Church of England, for example, we find this petition:

> Hear us as we remember those who have died in the faith of Christ...
> according to your promises,
> grant us with them a share in your eternal kingdom.

For most Anglicans, this does not affect the eternal destiny of the departed; it is rather like placing flowers on a grave. It is an act of love and remembrance, though some other believers might feel that such compassionate acts do bless the departed somehow. Other Christians avoid this altogether. There are many different views.

Judged by Mercy

The image of Jesus reaching out and holding the hand of the little dead girl, Jairus' daughter, shows that it is love and mercy that confront us, as well as holiness. The Greek Orthodox bishop, Kallistos Ware, says this:

> There is no terrorism in the Orthodox doctrine of God. Orthodox Christians do not cringe before Him in abject fear, but think of Him as *philanthropos*, the "lover of men"... Hell is not so much a place where God imprisons

man, as a place where man, by misusing his free will, chooses to imprison himself.

As Cardinal Cormac Murphy O'Connor wrote:

> But if I am to be judged by God, I am happy that I should be judged by One who came among us and lived our life just as it is – short, bitter and yet wonderful. It is as the Son of Man that God will examine us about our life. He has lived our life with sympathetic understanding of its fragility and unsolved enigmas...

A modern-day parable is told about the Day of Judgment. People are assembled on the plains of heaven. They wait for God to appear from behind a beautiful curtain. They are nervous and fearful and then, as time passes, they murmur and complain. "Who is he to judge us?" shouts one woman. She bares her arm to show the tattooed number she received at Auschwitz. Others join in this chorus and show their scars or tell their painful stories.

Then the curtain opens.

Silence.

Not a murmur.

From behind the curtain, a man steps forward. He has wounds in his hands and feet and a scar on his side.

He will judge us.

Mercy meets us: some will run to it; some will run away from it. Their own hearts have closed the door.

God is awesome and holy, and darkness cannot dwell with the light. Our God is a consuming fire and it is a fearful thing to fall into his hands.

His eternal love also reaches out to save. He came in Jesus and suffered for us. He has thrown out a lifeline for us.

There *is* a way of finding peace with God in this life, though, of knowing that we are accepted, forgiven and loved. This we must move on to, and the assurance Christians can have that their home is in heaven.

7

Peace with God

The New Testament declares that we can find peace with God, knowing that we are forgiven and accepted. This is because of what Jesus has done for us when we were powerless to save or justify ourselves before God.

Our Home is in Heaven

An early Christian writing from the late first century states that Christians form a "third race" that transcends nationality and genetic race:

> Every foreign country is their fatherland, and every fatherland is a foreign country... To put it shortly, what the soul is in the body, that the Christians are in the world. The soul is spread through all the members of the body, and Christians through all the cities of the world...
>
> (*The Epistle to Diognetus*)

This picks up on a text in the New Testament:

> Beloved, I beg you as sojourners and pilgrims, abstain from fleshly lusts which war against the soul.
>
> (1 Peter 2:11)

The image of Christians as strangers to the world is striking, and it is thus because their home is in heaven. Their new born spirits belong elsewhere.

In the Bible, Christians are said to live in heavenly places in their spirits:

> If then you were raised with Christ, seek those things which are above, where Christ is sitting at the right hand of God.
>
> (Colossians 3:1)

> But God, who is rich in mercy, because of His great love with which He loved us, even when we were dead in trespasses, made us alive together with Christ (by grace you have been saved), and raised us up together, and made us sit together in the heavenly places in Christ Jesus.
>
> (Ephesians 2:4–6)

The idea of being in heavenly places is made possible only by receiving Christ into our lives, and the power of the Holy Spirit.

New Birth

One of the images for finding this peace with God and new life in the Spirit is to be "born again" or to be "born from above". Jesus spoke to the Pharisee Nicodemus about his need for this:

> Most assuredly, I say to you, unless one is born again, he cannot see the kingdom of God.   (John 3:3)

When you read this passage in context it is clear that Jesus is not talking about reincarnation at all, but about a spiritual rebirth here and now in this life. This image is picked up and treated in the same way in 1 Peter.

> Blessed be the God and Father of our Lord Jesus Christ, who according to His abundant mercy has begotten us again to a living hope through the resurrection of Jesus Christ from the dead, to an inheritance incorruptible and undefiled and that does not fade away...   (1 Peter 1:3–4)

There are many other metaphors used for new life in Christ in the Bible, such as taking his yoke upon us or coming into the light, but this is a succinct and powerful image. It speaks of being given a gift, of something coming into us that we could not work up or manufacture ourselves. I have seen numerous people respond to preachers and go forward for prayer to receive Christ. I watch their faces as they go up, heavy, worried, burdened. Then they step back to their seats, lighter, eyes bright, and I can see that something new has entered their spirits. I can think back now to one of my congregation who was seeking for a while and then responded to a visiting preacher. She looked as though she had stepped into a new life. She sparkled!

I remember watching, also, an interview with two inmates of a prison in Northern Ireland. One was Catholic and the other was Protestant. They had hated each other until both had conversion experiences while in jail. Now they were brothers and their love for each other in Christ was palpable. Their religion had been nominal and even tribal in the past, but now it was a living relationship.

Many have a time of decision for Christ, a moment, a crisis experience. This can be very, very real. Not everyone does, though, for some are brought up in the faith and they imbibe the life as they go along. They find themselves in Christ without being able to name an exact time and date when it happened. It does not matter how we get there, so long as we know that we are there. If you fall asleep on a train journey, you will still get to your destination. You just will not remember when you entered the city that you were aiming for.

Hospitality

A story in the book of Genesis has Abraham offering hospitality to three strangers. This is an Eastern custom where the traveller is welcomed into the home (or the tent, in Abraham's case). The story can be found in Genesis 18:1–15. They bring a message from the Lord that Abraham's wife, Sarah, will have a child. The three men are recognised as angelic visitors, but later Christian tradition speculated that these were the three Persons of the Trinity, the Father, the Son and the Holy Spirit. The Eastern churches paint icons of this scene with the three angels seated around a table. Earlier versions were very homely with the figures of Abraham and Sarah rushing around in the background trying to rustle up some food. Later versions just have the three angels, looking serene. The iconographers all include one detail, however. They leave a space at the table open at the forefront of the picture. That is for each one of us. We are invited to enter the fellowship and sit with God.

Other Christian writers imagined the Persons of the Trinity as a round dance of love and joy, and humanity is invited to step into the circle, link arms and join in the dance. These are beautiful and moving images, but many, upon hearing this, object that they are not worthy. They have a sense of being sinful and flawed.

Knock! Knock!

Holman Hunt, the Pre-Raphaelite painter, produced the image of Jesus as *The Light of the World*. Here, the Lord stands outside a house, knocking on the door. He carries a lantern. The door has no handle on the outside – it is presumed that one exists only on the inside.

This image is based upon a text in the Bible where Jesus knocks on the door of our lives:

> Behold, I stand at the door and knock. If anyone hears My voice and opens the door, I will come in to him and dine with him, and he with Me. (Revelation 3:20)

This is a striking image and it tells us that we need to turn, to invite Jesus into our lives, to allow something to happen so that we can sit at the table or join in the dance.

The Cross

We cannot earn our own salvation by our own efforts. None of us are perfect; none of us are good enough or sinless. The diagram shows how people strive and try to bridge the gulf between ourselves and the holiness of God. Most other faiths are based upon this endeavour, to try their best to reach God. Christianity is different.

The cross of Christ is the bridge, for only his death could make up for human sin. There are many attempts to

explain how this can be, an idea called "the atonement". Basically, Jesus is seen as God living in the flesh, as more than a good man or a holy prophet. As the God-Man he offered his spotless, perfect life on the cross to make peace. He offered himself for the sins of humanity. It is like a judge stepping into the dock to pay the penalty himself. This is a moving and humbling example of the love of God.

Another idea is to see Jesus as joining God and humanity in friendship. He has taken away a partition and allowed God to come through and bless us.

This is the distinctive point about Christianity: God reaches down to raise us up to himself. It is not all left up to us. Our part is to bow the knee, submit our lives and receive him.

Justified and Sanctified

The act of atonement and the peace that is established is known as "justification". The sinner who repents and turns to Christ can stand justified before God even though we are not worthy in ourselves and have not done anything to deserve it. One way of understanding this is that God sees us through Christ. We are covered by him and his blood. There is more, though, for the Holy Spirit comes and applies the work of the cross in the human spirit, simultaneously regenerating it. There is a new, pure spirit within us. This is not by our own efforts but by grace, unmerited favour, a gift:

> Therefore, having been justified by faith, we have peace with God through our Lord Jesus Christ.   (Romans 5:1)

> For all have sinned and fall short of the glory of God, being justified freely by His grace through the redemption that is in Christ Jesus.   (Romans 3:23–24)

This act of justification is applied to the human spirit through the power of the indwelling Holy Spirit. It is not something totally external to us or a legal fiction. The Holy Spirit brings a new, spiritual birth and starts to fashion us in the image of Christ, a process that continues throughout our lives. This process is known as sanctification, "making holy". The two things, justification and sanctification, are both the work of the same Spirit and are one package deal. They cannot really be separated.

There have been disputes and debates throughout Christian history, particularly at the Reformation, over how these two things work. The Reformers tended to stress justification as a separate stage from sanctification; God declares us just in Christ as soon as we repent and then sanctification begins. The Catholics stressed the ongoing conversion of the soul and could not separate the act of justification from the process of sanctification and the gift of the Holy Spirit.

Both are needed and both involve the Holy Spirit. The danger with the Reformed position is that it can sound rather lax and open to abuse if we are not careful: "It does not matter how we live so long as we believe in Christ". Paul was attacked for this, too, and the Epistle of James attacks some followers of Paul who were distorting his message:

> You see then that a man is justified by works, and not by faith only. (James 2:24)

A genuine conversion, a real justification, meant that the Holy Spirit had come into a person's life and had made a fundamental change. This would be evident in a changed lifestyle and the fruits of good works. Trying to find peace with God by doing good works does not work; acts of charity that flow from a heart that has found peace are another matter.

Thankfully, as we live in more ecumenical times, theologians have been discussing these differences and are finding much more convergence. There was a momentous agreement between Lutheran theologians and Catholic scholars by the end of the second millennium where they agreed a form of words that saw justification and the sanctifying work of the Holy Spirit as one dynamic, resulting in the fruit of a changed life and good works. The present Pope, Benedict, then Cardinal Ratzinger, was eager to support this. It would be foolhardy to state that all differences have been settled, but we are well on the way.

Martin Luther had a profound experience of grace in the sixteenth century, after he had tried hard to live a Christian life with many rules, pilgrimages and rituals. These did not bring him the peace and acceptance he sought. After studying the New Testament, especially Romans, he felt that he was forgiven, that the gates of paradise had opened in his soul and he had entered. The peace he felt was profound. Later, in the eighteenth century, John Wesley heard a reading from the Epistle to the Romans and he said, "I felt my heart strangely warmed and I felt that I did trust in Christ, and Christ alone, for my salvation."

St Augustine of Hippo, centuries earlier, had heard a voice telling him to take up the book of the New Testament and read; he read Romans and found the same grace and peace.

This sense of forgiveness and peace with God is known as the inner witness of the Holy Spirit or assurance of salvation. Romans 8 explores this and says:

> The Spirit Himself bears witness with our spirit that we
> are children of God...   (Romans 8:16)

Or, look at the words of the hymn by Frances van Alstyne, "Blessed Assurance":

> Blessed assurance, Jesus is mine:
> O what a foretaste of glory divine!

Heir of salvation, purchase of God;
Born of His Spirit, washed in His blood.

This is the experience of many ordinary Christians; we can know peace with God because of what Jesus has done for us on the cross.

Set Apart

Paul uses the analogy of shopping for pots in his description of God's choosing of us:

> ... having believed, you were sealed with the Holy Spirit of promise, who is the guarantee of our inheritance until the redemption of the purchased possession, to the praise of His glory.   (Ephesians 1:13b–14)

In the markets of the Roman world you could ask for a pot to be marked with a seal before it was fired. It was then set aside for you and it would be "redeemed" when you came back to pay the price. The gift of the Holy Spirit has marked us with the seal of God's love and ownership. We are set apart until we finish this life and enter into full redemption in the glory and joy of heaven. In this life we will have struggles, doubts and uncertainties, but at the end is the prize. The indwelling Spirit is the guarantee of our hope and destiny. This setting apart is linked with the word for "saint". A saint is one set apart for Christ, and in that sense the New Testament can declare that all baptised believers are saints. The idea of a "saint" as a striking example and a really holy person grew up later; these individuals are looked up to as having reached the goal, and shine out as beacons to us on earth.

Running the Race

It is true that the work of justification and sanctification gives us peace and salvation, but we have to go on in obedience to Christ, walking with him and allowing the Spirit to heal us ready for glory. Paul describes this as running a race:

> I press toward the goal for the prize of the upward call of God in Christ Jesus.   (Philippians 3:14)

The Scriptures warn us that we can go astray or "make shipwreck" of our faith. The Catholic tradition speaks of the grace of "final perseverance" in that race. It reminds people to be humble and not presumptuous; we depend upon the grace of God all through our lives. There are debates about whether a person can lose their salvation once they have come to Christ. Some say, "No, once saved always saved." Others allow for a falling away (and this is so in the Catholic and the Reformed traditions). It is interesting that when Paul disciplined one wayward believer who had fallen into gross sin by sleeping with his stepmother, he excommunicated him but prayed that, though he would go through suffering, his soul would be saved (c.f. 1 Corinthians 5:4–5).

This suggests that it is very hard to lose salvation even if we turn against Christ. His grace is powerful and seeks us out throughout our lives. Indeed, many testify that they do stray, but come back to faith and are restored. If it is possible to lose one's salvation, then it is incredibly difficult and involves a real rejection without hope of repentance. As one minister put it, "I don't know if you can lose salvation, but I just know that I want to be in the kingdom and not outside it!" St Augustine stressed that God "does not desert" those who have been once justified by His grace "unless they desert Him first". Jesus stated:

> All that the Father gives to Me will come to Me, and the one who comes to Me I will by no means cast out.
>
> (John 6:37)

Once he has his mark upon us and the seal of love on our hearts, it is incredibly hard to lose him. The poet Francis Thompson spoke of the love of God as "the Hound of Heaven" pursuing him when he had wandered far from faith.

We are imperfect on this earth and we will sin, but we are encouraged to return again and again for forgiveness:

> If we confess our sins, He is faithful and just to forgive us our sins and to cleanse us from all unrighteousness.
>
> (1 John 1:9)

We live in imperfection, having the deposit of the Spirit, until we complete our lives. We live in between the ages in the "now" and "not yet" of salvation. We can have a pure, new spirit, but we live with temptations and clusters of emotions and drives from our fallen, mortal nature. The Scriptures promise that God will complete what he has begun and have us ready for heaven (Philippians 1:6).

In the Reformed tradition this will be in a moment of glory, in the twinkling of an eye, as we are forged and bathed in the purifying, healing fire of God's love, face to face when all the barriers are down. In the Catholic tradition it takes a period of time in the state of purgatory (whatever sense "time" has in the Beyond) but it gets to the same place, the bliss of heaven and the joyful vision of God.

The words of a verse of Charles Wesley's hymn "Love Divine" sum this up:

> Finish, then, Thy new creation;
> Pure and spotless let us be;
> Let us see Thy great salvation
> Perfectly restored in Thee:
> Changed from glory into glory,
> Till in heaven we take our place,
> Till we cast our crowns before Thee,
> Lost in wonder, love and praise.

Late Have I Loved Thee...

Speaking about "running the race" of faith might seem fine but what about someone who turns to Christ late in life, when elderly, sick or even on their death bed? Many such people do submit to him and call out for mercy and it is never too late. Jesus told a parable about the workers in the vineyard:

> For the kingdom of heaven is like a landowner who went out early in the morning to hire laborers for his vineyard. Now when he had agreed with the laborers for a denarius a day, he sent them into his vineyard. And he went out about the third hour and saw others standing idle in the marketplace, and said to them, "You also go into the vineyard, and whatever is right I will give you." So they went. Again he went out about the sixth and the ninth hour, and did likewise. And about the eleventh hour he went out and found others standing idle, and said to them, "Why have you been standing here idle all day?" They said to him,

"Because no one hired us." He said to them, "You also go into the vineyard, and whatever is right you will receive."

So when evening had come, the owner of the vineyard said to his steward, "Call the laborers and give them their wages, beginning with the last to the first." And when those came who were hired about the eleventh hour, they each received a denarius. But when the first came, they supposed that they would receive more; and they likewise received each a denarius. And when they had received it, they complained against the landowner, saying, "These last men have worked only one hour, and you made them equal to us who have borne the burden and the heat of the day." But he answered one of them and said, "Friend, I am doing you no wrong. Did you not agree with me for a denarius? Take what is yours and go your way. I wish to give to this last man the same as to you. Is it not lawful for me to do what I wish with my own things? Or is your eye evil because I am good?" So the last will be first, and the first last. For many are called, but few chosen.

(Matthew 20:1–16)

Those who worked for the last shift received the same pay as those who started early in the morning. It made lousy economics but excellent spirituality. The Father's love is equal for all, no matter when they turn to him. There will be regrets, of course, if people find forgiveness and salvation late in life, regrets about what they could have done with their lives to work for the kingdom. Yet, they are received and loved.

The Martyrs

A striking witness to the power of salvation and the peace with God that comes through Jesus is seen in those who knowingly face death for their faith. All through history Christian martyrs have shown great bravery and boldness before their murderers, and a peace that certainly passes understanding. They know a special touch of grace. This is evident in the first recorded martyr, Stephen, in the Acts of the Apostles. He died forgiving his enemies and he saw a vision of the risen Lord as his tormentors struck:

> When they heard these things they were cut to the heart, and they gnashed at him with their teeth. But he, being full of the Holy Spirit, gazed into heaven and saw the glory of God, and Jesus standing at the right hand of God, and said, "Look! I see the heavens opened and the Son of Man standing at the right hand of God!"
>
> Then they cried out with a loud voice, stopped their ears, and ran at him with one accord; and they cast him out of the city and stoned him. And the witnesses laid down their clothes at the feet of a young man named Saul. And they stoned Stephen as he was calling on God and saying, "Lord Jesus, receive my spirit." Then he knelt down and cried out with a loud voice, "Lord, do not charge them with this sin." And when he had said this, he fell asleep.   (Acts 7:54–60)

The Catholic monk Charles de Foucauld showed similar calm and peace when he was held at gunpoint and killed by a young terrorist in Algeria in the early twentieth century. The Lutheran pastor Dietrich Bonhoeffer was hanged by the Nazis in 1945. He was seen in his cell, just before being taken out for execution, praying fervently. The prison doctor recorded:

> Through the half open door of one of the huts I saw Pastor Bonhoeffer still in his prison clothes, kneeling in

fervent prayer to the Lord his God. The devotion and evident conviction of being heard that I saw in the prayer of
this intensely captivating man, moved me to the depths.

Again, during the closing months of the war, some
Carthusian monks were imprisoned and tortured for hiding Jews. One of the brothers shouted to his confrères in
other cells:

> Be strong, what are you waiting for? We must prepare
> ourselves! Don't you know what awaits us?

An early martyr, St Ignatius of Antioch, was on his way to
be executed in Rome in the early second century. He wrote
to the believers in Rome urging them not to be upset for
him but to rejoice that he was about to enter heaven:

> ... in me there is left no spark of desire for mundane
> things, but only a murmur of living water that whispers
> within me, "Come to the Father". There is no pleasure for
> me in any meats that perish, or in the delights of this
> life...   (Ignatius, *Epistle to the Romans*)

The grace that touches the martyrs opens the glory and
hope of heaven for them. They know whom they have
believed and he is faithful to receive them.

Most of us are not called to face anything like their fate,
but all of us can have that hope within us: "We must prepare ourselves. Don't you know what awaits us?"

The next chapter will explore that hope in all its riches.

If, reading this, you feel that you have not made a personal commitment to Jesus Christ and that you do not
know peace with God, then, when you are ready, recite a
prayer such as this:

Lord Jesus Christ,
I turn to you and ask for mercy.
I admit that I have sinned and that you died for me.
I thank you for this and ask you to come into my life by
the power of your Holy Spirit.
Come in to free me, to cleanse me, to forgive me.
Amen.

Ideally, seek out a believer whom you trust and pray this
with them.

8

The Hope of Heaven

What might an afterlife be like? Where might it be located and would it follow very different laws of physics? Would there be room for everyone? If it goes on and on for ever, wouldn't people get bored?

These are the sorts of question people ask about heaven. This chapter will try to answer them and explore the vibrant Christian hope of heaven.

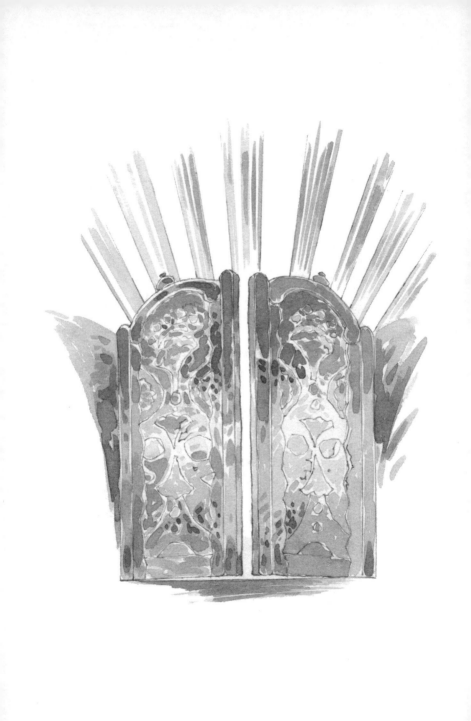

What is Heaven Like?

Various answers are suggested to this. One, offered in the nineteenth century, was "It's like eating *foie gras* to the sound of trumpets." A more recent one was, "It's like watching cricket with the volume turned down as you wear headphones playing choral Evensong."

Both of these suggestions have their distinct limitations. It all depends if you like *foie gras* and brass bands, or cricket and choral Evensong. If you are an unsporty vegetarian who is into folk music and flutes, then it would be pretty miserable!

George Orwell complained that the Christian heaven sounded too much like choir practice in a jeweller's shop. The robed choirboys, high-pitched notes and tacky gold ornaments sounded stuffy and dull to him.

The above suggestions are human, limited analogies. They offer comparisons based upon projections of what the person really enjoys (or dislikes, in the case of Orwell). If heaven is a form of bliss and infinite happiness, then what might it be like? Just imagine...or, then again... There is no harm in this if we realise the limitations. We are trying to visualise the Beyond, to tame transcendence by tying it up in our mundane concepts. It is rather like the dying patient who held the hand of the hospital chaplain and whispered, "This heaven...is it a bit like going on holiday to Southend?" Apparently, that is where he had gone as a child, and it was logged in his mind as an image of joy. Yes, it is something like going on holiday as a child to Southend, but it is also something far, far grander than that.

Just as a blind person cannot really describe what a beautiful sunset looks like, or a person who sees in monochrome cannot describe the wonder of a rainbow, so too we cannot do justice to the hope of heaven with our descriptions. It is something beyond us. To hark back to the Scriptures, it will come as a surprise:

> Eye has not seen, nor ear heard,
> Nor have entered into the heart of man
> The things which God has prepared for those who love Him. (1 Corinthians 2:9)

Again, Paul says that we might "know the love of Christ which passes knowledge" (Ephesians 3:19a) or that we might have "the peace of God which surpasses all understanding" (Philippians 4:7). Paul speaks of a time when he was granted a vision of heaven and the glory of God:

> And I know such a man – whether in the body, or out of the body I do not know, God knows – how he was caught up into Paradise and heard inexpressible words, which it is not lawful for a man to utter. (2 Corinthians 12:3–4)

God is a mystery and all talk about heaven is transcendent. Any attempt to speak of God himself must be analogous and limited. As the Dominican friar Timothy Radcliffe says in his book *I Call You Friends*, "The glory of God escapes our words. The mystery breaks our little ideologies… Does that mean that we can just be silent? No, because monasteries are not just places of silence but of song. We have to find ways of singing, at the limits of language, at the edge of meaning."

The renowned medieval friar Thomas Aquinas once said that our words about God are allowed as they are adequate (*adequatio*) but they are limited. We cannot capture the divine or tie God down. Aquinas wrote volumes of complex and erudite learning, but he was granted a vision of the glory of God, which brought him to silence. He declared that all he had written before this was like straw in comparison. We taste the Beyond and eat humble pie.

It is interesting to sift through the accounts of NDE experiencers as they seek to describe their brush with the Beyond. It is indescribable beauty or warmth, bright light or verdant countryside that is nothing like we experience. It is all alive, so wonderfully alive with colours that can be felt as well as seen. Remember the stuttering exclamations of George Ritchie as he tried to sum up the Being of Light as "the most magnificent being [he had] ever known..."

NDEs are fascinating and might give us insights and glimpses of the nature of heaven. There seems to be some sort of shape and form even if it transcends anything known on earth. Of course, we do not know if the initial experiences of the departed are temporary, a caring nursery environment created to aid their crossing over. So, familiar garden scenes or trees or places might be a hallucination that warps into the more magnificent forms and contours of heaven once the spirit has readjusted. Think, on a more mundane level, of the weird scenes at the close of Stanley Kubrick's *2001, A Space Odyssey*. There the astronaut finds himself in a grand bedroom and awaits his transformation into a Star Child, a new species. He is prepared, step by step, as his mind has to cope with total newness.

To tell an amusing story, an inner-city priest I knew woke up in the early hours to cries of "Gloria! Gloria!" He thought he must have died and gone to heaven and how kind it was of God to recreate his own room to acclimatise him at first. Then it dawned on him; the cries were from a drunk across the road who was trying to rouse his girl-friend, Gloria!

What Sort of Body?

A similar question to "What is heaven like?" is "What sort of resurrection body will we have?" Again, we handle mysteries of the Beyond. Paul teaches that there will be a form we inhabit, a spiritual body that does not conform to the laws of physics that we know now. It is a higher form than anything on earth, and he makes this point by comparing it with the heavenly bodies, referring to an idea of grandeur and hierarchy among them. The earthly body is inferior:

> There are also celestial bodies and terrestrial bodies; but the glory of the celestial is one, and the glory of the terrestrial is another. There is one glory of the sun, another glory of the moon, and another glory of the stars; for one star differs from another star in glory.
>
> (1 Corinthians 15:40–41)

He clearly sees that the resurrection body is of a higher order and is more real than this frail, mortal body. We will not be mere spooks or bundles of ethereal protoplasm that supposedly emanate from mediums. We will have more depth and reality than we now have.

> The body is sown in corruption, it is raised in incorruption. It is sown in dishonor, it is raised in glory.
>
> (1 Corinthians 15:42b–43a)

To ask what it will look like, to ask if we are a certain age or if we will have the same kind of hair (or lack of it!), is to miss the point of the majesty of the new creation. It is beyond us. I recall one prominent Bible teacher who went on a preaching tour of Eastern Europe. One small church group had a strict teaching about make-up and adorning the hair for women. One of the women had a new hair-style, following the fashions of the day, and the elders tut-tutted. The preacher was asked his opinion. He was silent and thought for a moment and then he had a whiff of inspiration: "Not to worry. In the resurrection, everything will be perfect!" he replied.

Let us rest in reverent agnosticism about the details but affirm the reality and the hope with all our faith.

Where is Heaven?

Heaven is not really supposed to be up above us. In ancient times, primitive peoples probably thought that the sky was the domain of the gods. They did not know how it worked or what was up there. They often thought about the world as a three-storey place with the gods upstairs, people in the middle and the dead beneath in the Underworld. They knew no better. Ideas of heaven go beyond this in the Scriptures and in Christian tradition, however. Heaven is not "up" or "down" but within, some-how. It is in another dimension or plane of reality. We live in a three-dimensional world of length, breadth and height. A fourth dimension can be added, that of time. Try to imagine what it would be like living a two-dimensional existence in Flatland. We could not imagine living with extra dimensions. Heaven bursts out beyond our four dimensions in the space/time continuum of our physical universe into a multifarious series of levels that we cannot comprehend. Maybe it is a little like the various levels in the average computer game. You have to complete one before you can access another. The "world" you inhabit in the next level is different and the rules are totally new. Heaven is a step beyond, only accessed when this life is completed.

It is true that we still tend to use height language for God and heaven – "God above" and so on. Height suggests power and greatness, the best. Think of the gold-medal winners at the Olympics. They are stood on the top step of the podium. The best-selling song is "Top of the Pops" in the same way. To say that a head teacher is above everyone in a school is not meant to be taken literally; they are not flying overhead but they have the authority. Just so, height imagery for God and heaven suggests supremacy, authority and majesty. What about the ascension story? Acts 1:9–11 relates the experience of seeing the risen Lord rise up and be hidden by a cloud. He left this plane to return to the Father.

> Now when He had spoken these things, while they watched, He was taken up, and a cloud received him from their sight. (Acts 1:9)

I have no doubt that the disciples had a very real visionary experience but it symbolised all the things mentioned above. Neither did Jesus float up and up and away like a rocket. The cloud that obscured him from sight was a symbol for the glory of God; this symbol appears several times in the Bible. He was embraced and received into glory, moving onto a different plane of reality.

In heaven our known laws of physics break down and new ones apply. In our world, everything begins and has an ending. The principle of entropy, of the petering out of energy, applies. It is inescapable. However, in heaven this is not so. Entropy is dethroned. Perhaps mathematics can give us a hint of this reversal in the infinity of numbers. There is not only the number π with its endless list of numbers after its decimal point, but the very infinity of numbers themselves. To illustrate this, play the following game:

Think of the biggest number you can.
Add one.
Multiply by two.
Think of the smallest number you can.
Take away one.
Divide by two.
And so on, and so on *ad infinitum*.

Perhaps life in heaven reverses some of what we experience now. We do not grow tired but go from strength to strength. Joy does not fade but grows ever stronger. If we think of the spiritual experiences we can have on earth, we catch a hint of this. Spending time in prayer and worship in the presence of God rejuvenates and refreshes. Hence Isaiah's poetic charge:

> But those who wait on the Lord
> Shall renew their strength;
> They shall mount up with wings like eagles,
> They shall run and not be weary,
> They shall walk and not faint. (Isaiah 40:31)

Heaven cannot be found by the most searching telescope, rocket or space probe. If it is outside the box of our physical universe then nothing physical can ever find it. It is not on either side of the Milky Way or down the farthest, deepest black hole. Paul reminds us "flesh and blood cannot inherit the kingdom of God" (1 Corinthians 15:50). Heaven is tuned into spiritually and it is our spirits that have access, not our mortal bodies. The doorway lies within us.

Human knowledge and imagination is wonderful but limited. Richard Dawkins admits this even with his advocacy of the advance and hegemony of science. He states that our minds run limited software that constructs a virtual reality or a model of how the universe works. We work with a model of reality, and not actual reality. The only way we can get "outside the universe" is in the sense of "putting a model of the universe inside our skulls". If we cannot really understand the physical world, how can we capture the spiritual in our conceptual nets? The cosmos becomes ever more slippery and mysterious, too, as light seems to behave as waves and as particles. Quantum physics breaks laws down into random chaos and subatomic dances. Science has to court the language of metaphor and paradox as well as religion.

Heaven can be accessed by intuition, by metaphor and by poetry and the spirit. Faith reaches out and hopes; faith believes and trusts even when it cannot prove QED and demonstrate under a microscope.

The question "Will there be room for everyone?" also breaks down into nonsense if the laws of this other dimension are totally different. Shape, form and substance work differently. We also wonder what will happen to time. If time is bound up with the physical universe, what sort of time is there in heaven? Maybe it ceases to be. On the other hand, NDE experiencers talk about things moving at lightning speed there as though everything is much more alive and alert. Their awareness of movement on earth is like something in slow motion. It might be that there is no time in heaven or a different sort of time, akin to a different sort of shape and form. We do not know. It is like fish imagining what it would be like to leave the water and to live in the atmosphere.

Heaven is Where Jesus is

All the speculations and mind games we have been playing up until now in this chapter are interesting but rather empty. Heaven is more than a place, another dimension and a new way of being. It is where Jesus is. It is where the glory dwells. It is about a vision of beauty and the blessed. Theologians speak of the "beatific vision", the glorious goal that awaits the redeemed. Going to heaven is not about endless life or joy, but about an endless relationship. It is being in the presence of God and basking in his glory. People who, like Paul, tell stories of having visited heaven briefly report beautiful singing and rising praise that brings joy and life. People do tell of such experiences, whether NDEs or visions granted while alive. I have heard a New Zealand minister relate his vision, where he could feel and see vivid colours and see sounds that vibrated with life. Of course, he was trying to put into human words things and experiences that could not really be uttered. Above and beyond all, though, was the presence and vision of God. One word from the risen Jesus was like a roaring waterfall or a mighty wind that brought silence and a sense of unspeakable joy. A beatific vision, a longing that is hinted at in every glimpse of beauty on earth from a sunset to nature to a baby's smile. It is total beauty, raw life. Glimpses of this can be caught in this life; I heard of a woman who awoke one morning to hear incredible, enchanted, beautiful singing around her. This was the music of paradise. She was aware of a presence and, as she sat up to look, it dispersed, moved, vanished. Sadly, a day or so later, her husband died suddenly. This little glimpse of the beauty of heaven touched her as a preparation.

This scotches any argument that if there is a heaven then we would end up dreadfully bored. Images of people sitting on clouds with little harps are tawdry and unbiblical. If we live in a spiritual plane with different laws of motion and reality, in the presence of the living God, then we are swimming in Life itself. One image of the blessing of heaven in the Bible is a river of life:

> And he showed me a pure river of water of life, clear as crystal, proceeding from the throne of God and of the Lamb. In the middle of its street, and on either side of the river, was the tree of life, which bore twelve fruits, each tree yielding its fruit every month. The leaves of the tree were for the healing of the nations.   (Revelation 22:1–2)

Some believers have claimed visions of visiting heaven and splashing in the waters of this beautiful river with Jesus, laughing and jumping. The river felt alive, energising, a force of divinity. The evangelist Dutch Sheets, for example, reported this in his *The River of God*. He describes being in the water with Jesus:

> When my head went under and I accidentally breathed in, the water didn't choke me as water typically does. Instead of going into my lungs, causing me to gag and choke, it flowed throughout my entire body, bringing refreshment and vitality. It was indeed, the river of *life*...
>
> As people were moving in and out of the water, I saw a lady diseased with cancer. Jesus looked at me, smiling. He

said rather matter-of-factly, "Well, go heal her." I walked to her and put my hand on her. As I did, the Lord moved behind me and placed His hand in the middle of my back. When He did, power went from Him, through me and into this lady, healing her. We then went back to playing in the river...

No, we won't get bored. Paul speaks about moving "from glory to glory" (2 Corinthians 3:18) and of moving on toward the goal:

Forgetting those things which are behind and reaching forward to those things which are ahead, I press toward the goal for the prize of the upward call of God in Christ Jesus.   (Philippians 3:13–14)

The goal might seem to be the end of the moving on, but some early Christian writers supposed that the dynamic, life-abounding nature of heaven could not be static. We would always be on the move from glory to glory, ever venturing deeper in, closer to God and reaching forward. It is an amazing, dynamic journey into a beautiful mystery as Jesus leads us by the hand, like Jairus' daughter.

We can catch a glimpse of this dynamism in the words of John Newton's hymn *Amazing Grace*:

When we've been there ten thousand years,
Bright shining as the sun,
We've no less days to sing God's praise
Than when we first began.

I heard the testimony of a very ill patient recently that summed up the hope of heaven as a beatific vision. Friends had prayed with him, claiming healing for him and believing in the power of prayer. Left all alone and unsure, the patient felt a presence in the room. He turned his head and looked. There was the Lord, resplendent, majestic, aglow with light. He looked into Jesus' eyes and he knew that if he died, he was in those hands, and he felt an incredible peace descend upon him. There is a time to die, to cross over, when prayers will not revive us and keep us here.

I saw this only too clearly when ministering to a woman dying of cancer. Many Christian brothers and sisters prayed for her and believed for her healing. I must admit that some of the bedside prayer sessions were very powerful and a strong sense of the presence of God descended. She looked more radiant and perky as a result and I certainly would never decry the power of God to heal. However, she steadily declined and slipped into unconsciousness as her body started to shut itself down. Some were despondent that their prayers had not been answered, but we have to let go and hand people over to the Father. Our love for them wants to hold on, but we have to offer them up and place them into his hands. There is a time.

Many clergy and medical staff can testify to the rapture, joy and release that can come to dying patients just before they expire. Some are comatose or drugged into unconsciousness, of course, and some struggle with guilt and fight, but many find a release, a deep peace, towards the end and this is a sacred, moving experience to behold. Some years ago Dr Leslie Weatherhead collected a number of such stories and many he had experienced in his book *Life Begins at Death*. He wrote this:

But I have sat at the bedside of a man who was dying and who was conscious to the end. He gripped my hand and I must have gripped his more tightly than I thought I was doing, for he said, "Don't hold me back. I can see through the gates. It's marvellous."

.If you have seen, as I have, a woman so ill that she couldn't lift her head from the pillow, if you had seen her sit up, her eyes open with tremendous delight, and joy in her face, if you had heard her call the name of a beloved husband who had been dead twenty years, you would find it strangely convincing. People may say it was probably a hallucination, or a trick of the brain. All I can say is that it was very convincing to the onlooker that she was really in touch with the beloved dead and that he was coming back to welcome her.

Similar stories abound, also of visions of angels and of Jesus.

This can be so of people who are not seemingly termi- nally ill or in hospital. John Wessells tells that his little boy sang his own songs about heaven before he became ill, and a friend of mine reported that his mother had sud- denly died peacefully in her sleep, after talking, transfixed, about heaven to her home group.

To be in heaven is to be with Jesus, the risen Jesus who is alive more gloriously than anything that we can imag- ine. Read these words from the opening chapter of Revelation as John was granted a vision of the majesty of the risen Lord:

Then I turned to see the voice that spoke with me. And having turned I saw seven golden lampstands, and in the midst of the seven lampstands One like the Son of Man, clothed with a garment down to the feet and girded about the chest with a golden band. His head and hair were white like wool, as white as snow, and His eyes like a flame of fire; His feet were like fine brass, as if refined in a furnace, and His voice as the sound of many waters; He had in His right hand seven stars, out of His mouth went a sharp two-edged sword, and His countenance was like the sun shining in its strength. And when I saw Him, I fell at His feet as dead. But He laid His right hand on me, saying to me, "Do not be afraid; I am the First and the Last. I am He who lives, and was dead, and behold, I am alive forevermore. Amen. And I have the keys of Hades and of Death." (Revelation 1:12–18)

The Bible and Heaven

We have seen that the Scriptures speak of resurrection, of being in the glory, of eternal life. We have seen that a river of life is imagined, of light and unutterable bliss. There is also healing and peace and all tears are wiped away:

God Himself will be with them and will be their God. And God will wipe away every tear from their eyes; there shall be no more death, nor sorrow, nor crying. There shall be no more pain, for the former things have passed away.
(Revelation 21:3b–4)

Beyond this, we have symbols of bliss, holiness and majesty. If we search through Revelation 4 and 5 then these images are heaped upon one another to amazing effect.

- There are sounds – there was an angelic voice like a trumpet blast. There were thunderings, lightnings and voices from the throne of God. There was heavenly singing from angels and the saints.

- The song of the seraphim, the heavenly creatures near the throne of God, is that heard by the prophet Isaiah (see Isaiah 6) at his call: "Holy, Holy, Holy..." The thrice-holy hymn, the Trisagion, is seen as praise to the glorious Trinity.
- There are wonderful creatures, the seraphim or the "living beings" around the throne, with wings and covered with eyes all over their bodies. (In Isaiah's vision they cover their faces with their wings so that they do not stare into the glory of God as they are so close to him.)
- There is movement as the elders cast down their crowns before the throne in worship.
- There are sights such as the radiant throne, the rainbow, jewels, a clear, crystal sea, seven lamps of fire, and the wondrous Lamb. The objects are symbols of royalty, majesty, power and purity.
- There is smell – the delightful aroma of pleasant incense offered from golden bowls: the prayers of the saints.
- There is music, the old song of the elders and the living creatures praising the Creator, and the new song of the redeemed, praising the Lamb who was slain. Only humanity can sing that song, and not the angels. Indeed, Scripture tells us that the angels long to look into the mystery of the gospel (1 Peter 1:12). The blood of Jesus has opened heaven and people of every race and tribe and nation are assembled together. They share the same Holy Spirit, they are washed in the blood of the Lamb and they stand as one in all their glorious variety.

These symbols and descriptions should not be taken as a series of snapshots of heaven. They are symbols that are using analogy, as human beings have to do. Heaven is something akin to what is described, but only more real and brighter still. Don't get me wrong: heaven is not itself a symbol. It is a reality, but we can speak of it only in symbols. The symbols hint at something and try to utter the unutterable. Heaven is holy, joyful, beautiful and full of the rich majesty of God. The Scriptures and our songs try to convey this. The actual thing is more blessed and it is waiting for us as a surprise.

The words of the hymn *Jerusalem the Golden*, taken from the verses of St Bernard of Cluny, capture the wonder, majesty and mystery of the hope of heaven:

I know not, O I know not
what social joys are there,
what radiancy of glory,
what light beyond compare...

They stand, those halls of Sion,
conjubilant with song,
and bright with many an angel,
and all the martyr throng:
the Prince is ever in them,
the daylight is serene,
the pastures of the blessed
Are decked with glorious sheen...

O sweet and blessed country,
when shall I see thy face?
O sweet and blessed country,
when shall I win they grace?
Exult, O dust and ashes!
The Lord shall be thy part:
his only, his for ever,
thou shalt be, and thou art!

(Words: Bernard of Cluny, 1145; trans. John Mason Neale, 1851.)

Let John Bunyan have the final word, as his pilgrim reaches heaven:

… "I see myself now at the end of my journey, my toilsome days are ended. I am going now to see that head that was crowned with thorns, and that face that was spit upon for me.

I have formerly lived by hear-say and faith, but now I go where I shall live by sight, and shall be with him, in whose company I delight myself.

I have loved to hear my Lord spoken of, and wherever I have seen the print of his shoe in the earth, there I have coveted to set my foot too.

His name has been to me as a civet-box, yea, sweeter than all perfumes. His voice to me has been most sweet, and his countenance I have more desired than they that have most desired the light of the sun. His word I did use to gather for my food, and for his antidotes against my faintings. He has held me, and I have kept me from mine iniquities: yea, my steps hath he strengthened in his way."

Now while he was thus in discourse his countenance changed, his strong men bowed under him, and after he had said, "Take me, for I am come unto thee", he ceased to be seen of them.

But glorious it was, to see how the open region was filled with horses and chariots, with trumpeters and pipers, with singers, and players on stringed instruments, to welcome the pilgrims as they went up and followed one another in at the beautiful Gate of the City.

(John Bunyan, *The Pilgrim's Progress*)

9

Comfort

"Comfort, yes, comfort My people!"
says your God.   *(Isaiah 40:1)*

Despite the vibrant, real hope of life after death and the glory of heaven in the Christian faith, there is still a pain of loss and a necessary process of grieving. To feel sadness and to shed tears is not a lack of faith, but a natural human response.

Pain and Loss

Bereavement is a very real and powerful process. We will feel down and devastated, lost and confused for a time. There is a long-term process of readjustment that goes on. Experts say that this runs, on average, for the best part of two years if it is not interrupted or blocked in any way. There is a path through initial shock, then denial, to the expression of grief. Failure to reach the stage of grief will bring withdrawal, confusion and anger.

We need to honestly feel the pain of the loss. We have spoken much in this book about Christian hope and the joy of heaven. All those things are true and helpful, but they should not try to mask very real, human pain. It is right to rejoice at a believer's funeral, that they are in heaven. However, we also need to express sorrow at the same time. A Christian funeral should be a bitter-sweet affair.

Some time ago, I read the words of an agnostic journalist who had attended a memorial service for one of his media friends at a London church. The deceased had been a committed Christian, and the tenor of the service was joyful, celebrating his life and his God. The agnostic could appreciate some of this, but he felt like standing up and shouting, "But he's dead! He's gone! And I'm sad!" Christian hope must not mask the expression of grief.

It is natural for tears to flow, and for a great sense of loss to be felt. If God had not put the gift of love in human hearts then we would not feel its flip side of the pain of loss. We cannot have the one without the other. There can be a sense of peace, a touch of joy through the Holy Spirit during a bereavement, but there is also pain. The rawness, the savagery of that pain can heal, but a degree of pain will always be felt. That must be so if we really cared for someone.

When bereavement comes, even to a strong believer, there will be shock and disturbance. We would not be human otherwise. C.S. Lewis wrote many great things about the Christian faith, helping many to understand it and to come to faith for themselves. He taught and argued passionately for the resurrection and for life after death. When his wife, Joy Gresham, died from cancer, he was devastated like anyone else. He struggled and fought and nearly lost his faith for a time.

I read recently about the loss suffered by an Indian evangelist, Dr D.G.S. Dhinakaran. He lost his beloved daughter, Angel, when she was barely a teenager. She died in a car crash. He keeps a picture of her in his office and he says, "Every time I see my dear daughter's picture, my heart is broken into pieces. Tears gush forth from my eyes like a spring…"

The pain never leaves. This is the confession of a devout man of God who leads evangelistic rallies and healing missions, bringing hope to many. He is allowed to be human and feel the pain, and rightly so.

John Wessells, whom I mentioned in an earlier chapter with his ministry to comatose and head injury patients, describes how he lost his first child, his little boy. Cancer took him after much prayer, treatment and suffering. John was plunged into grief and the pain of loss; he knew God's presence in all this, holding him up. In fact, when the boy passed away he looked up and reached out as though he had seen Jesus or the angels coming for him. An incredible peace and presence filled that room. But the pain was still there. John Wessells had lost his little boy. In one of his own songs, he laments this loss to this day, deeply missing him.

Why?

We live in a fallen world where things are not as they should be. There is pain and suffering here that will one day be rectified. Paul puts it this way:

> For I consider that the sufferings of this present time are not worthy to be compared with the glory which shall be revealed in us... For we know that the whole creation groans and labors with birth pangs together until now.
>
> (Romans 8:18, 22)

We just do not have all the answers this side of the grave. Theologians talk about an "eschatological realisation" of the problem of suffering, from the Greek "eschatos" meaning "last". This affirms that we do not understand now, but we shall one day. All shall be revealed and be made well in the kingdom of heaven.

There is a deep truth about the statement, "A time to be born...a time to die..." (Ecclesiastes 3:2) and there is a sense in which the ending of any life must be in the hands of, and by permission of, almighty God. "No one has power over the spirit to retain the spirit, and no one has power in the day of death" (Ecclesiastes 8:8).

Yet we rage against the wisdom of this in the face of tragedies and murders, or children who die before what should be their time. That is only honest and human. Perhaps, too, we must remember that this world and human beings are given a good measure of freedom by God. He gives his creation space to be and does not step in like some kind of Superman or moral policeman every step of the way. We have responsibility for our actions.

A friend of mine lost a baby through cot death some years back. In her grief and anger she yelled at God,

shouting at him for taking away her child. A wise coun-
sellor comforted her and said this: "Maybe God did not
take her, but he has *received* her." God might not always
will a death, like some sterile fate, but he allows it and is
there to receive the departed one. Mysteries; we handle
mysteries, and we have to live with the paradox that life
and death are in God's hands but human free will also
comes into play in a fallen, fragile world. How can we
affirm one and the other at the same time? It is a paradox,
akin to scientists seeing the behaviour of light as waves
and particles in different ways, at the same time. It is
mind-boggling. We do not have all the answers this side of
the grave. To quote Paul again:

> For now we see in a mirror, dimly, but then face to face.
> Now I know in part, but then I shall know just as I am
> known. (1 Corinthians 13:12)

Through the Valley of the Shadow of Death...

There can be special graces, visions, anointings, touches
of the Spirit that really help some people to climb out of a
hole of grief. These are consolations as we walk through
the valley of the shadow of death. Another story from the
Indian church concerns a man who had lost three baby
boys, one after another. He was crushed, and he found his
wife expired; her life had given way with the grief. He tried
to throw himself down a well and survived. He tried to
take poison, and had locked himself in his room, ready to
do so, when a sense of the presence of God came upon
him that took away the fear and the crushing sadness. He
was able to rebuild his life and walk hand in hand with
God through the valley of the shadow of death. ("Yea,

though I walk through the valley of the shadow of death, I will fear no evil; For You are with me; Your rod and Your staff, they comfort me" [Psalm 23:4].) He was given no answers, though; not now, not this side of eternity. God's presence was, and is, enough. Then we know that there is light at the end of the tunnel.

But let's not forget that the Christian hope is that we shall see our loved ones again:

> For the Lord Himself will descend from heaven with a shout, with the voice of an archangel, and with the trumpet of God. And the dead in Christ will rise first. Then we who are alive and remain shall be caught up together with them in the clouds to meet the Lord…
>
> (1 Thessalonians 4:16–17)

Most people do not receive these extraordinary graces, but there is a common grace that is sufficient. By seeking the Lord, by prayer, by the consolation of the Scriptures and close friendships, we will be strengthened. The rest of this chapter gives some tips and helpful hints to walk the path of bereavement, hand in hand with God.

Scriptures

Paul tells us to be washed in the word (Ephesians 5:26) and also that our minds can be renewed (Romans 12:2). Isaiah tells us to seek the Lord to gain renewed strength:

> But those who wait on the Lord
> Shall renew their strength;
> They shall mount up with wings like eagles,
> They shall run and not be weary,
> They shall walk and not faint.   (Isaiah 40:31)

We are tripartite beings, made up of spirit, soul and body. The spirit is the deepest part of our beings, the part that communes with God and lives for ever. Our "soul" means the mind and emotions, the feeling/thinking part of us. What happens in the spirit will affect the rest. Despite having awful struggles and depressions in the soul area, for very good reasons, if we feed the spirit, we shall rise up and gain new strength. This is still part of a healing process, as we withdraw and weep and grieve, but it is like medicine that helps us grow stronger day by day.

Take Scriptures as your medicine. Read your Bible even when you do not feel like it; listen to teaching from spiritual men and women. Soak in this like having a long bath. Wash in the word. A good soak always does us good!

The following Scriptures are just a selection, a useful and handy list to meditate upon, maybe taking one per day. Let these sink deep into your hearts and release God's power and strength. Take Psalm 119:50, for example:

> This is my comfort in my affliction,
> For Your word has given me life.

And also verse 92:

> Unless Your Law had been my delight,
> I would then have perished in my affliction.

As we draw near to him, God's Spirit can bring a consolation that we could not produce ourselves.

Scriptures to Encourage
- 2 Corinthians 1:3
- Romans 15:6

- Psalm 84:12
- Isaiah 2:5
- Isaiah 30:18
- Isaiah 51:12
- Isaiah 61:2
- Isaiah 66:13
- Psalm 91:1–2
- Psalm 139:1–3, 7–8, 11–12
- Luke 1:78–79
- 2 Corinthians 7:5–6
- Philemon 7
- Colossians 4:11
- Ephesians 6:22

Friends

Though a bereaved person needs to withdraw to some extent, they do not need to be completely cut off. They need friends and regular contact. Too often people stay away as they do not know what to say, and this can be very painful to bear. One does not need to talk deeply about the bereavement. A bereaved person wants touch, a listening ear, human contact and warmth as well as some personal space. Holding the hand, making tea, sharing a cake, listening to the feelings of someone who is down and misses their loved one dearly and saying little in return – that is all that is needed, beyond some prayer fellowship and ministry where appropriate and when requested.

Scripture says that a good friend is a delight to the heart:

Ointment and perfume delight the heart,
And the sweetness of a man's fiend gives delight by merry
counsel.   (Proverbs 27:9)

Proverbs declares that a true friend can be more support-
ive than a sibling, sometimes:

> A friend loves at all times,
> And a brother is born for adversity.   (Proverbs 17:17)

It is important that the bereaved do not cut themselves off
from spiritual fellowship, but many do not understand
their reluctance to come to a church service when they
tread through the early days of the bereavement process.
The bereaved find that they can be very vulnerable in a
large crowd. They might become tearful and start to sob
and become very awkward and embarrassed. Give people
space, have one or two visit at home and pray with them.
Have a home communion if that can be arranged. This
sense of unease will pass.

That is not to encourage any "Job's Comforters", by the
way. Those friends of Job shot their mouth off too quickly
and whined on about matters they did not understand in
their inadequacy. Do not judge or lecture any bereaved
person, even if you might be right. They cannot take it.
They are too crushed. And when they ask "Why?" they do
not expect a response. There isn't one; life is like that, the
world is fallen. Instead, offer the silence of companionship
and the squeeze of a hand. Stand with them, as Christ
stood with us in our condition, going to the cross for us.
No answers this side of the grave, but a God who rose
again and loves us with an everlasting love. He invites us
to take his hand.

Cheap answers can do much harm, too. I know of a girl
who lost her father. A minister told her: "Perhaps God
loved your daddy so much that he just had to take him to
be with him." The minister meant well, but what a disas-

ter! What distorted image of God did that impress upon that young mind? It was certainly not one of trust.

Prayer Tips and Things to Do

When John Wessells mourned his son's death, this is how he felt:

> I was entering a new world. I've never known such pain, or such peace. Some things are too deep to be voiced.

Some things *are* too deep to be voiced. When we find it hard to know how we feel, or how to express it, having something to do, something physical to actually get hold of and do something with, can be very helpful. This might seem almost by rote, but things that we do in this way can go deep and build a foundation to rest upon when our emotions are all over the place.

If a believer has the gift of speaking in tongues, then this is an excellent way of raising our hearts to God when we cannot put things into words. This allows people to express deep feelings, bypassing reason (c.f. St Paul's advice in Romans 8:26–27). Pray in this way each morning and evening for about fifteen minutes at a time. There will be an uplifting and a refreshing.

Christian devotion has a number of "things to do", also, that involve gestures or symbols.

(a) Lighting candles

The simplest is to light a prayer candle. This might be in a prayer corner at church or at home. A candle suggests the light of hope, the resurrection. Sit and look at it flickering away and try to say a prayer, or just be still.

(b) Holding crosses

Holding crosses are becoming popular across the denominations. These are small, plain crosses that are shaped to fit easily into the hand. Some find great comfort in gripping one of these when they are too upset to say much, too numb in their feelings, or very frightened. The suffering and the dying can find solace in these, too. I know of one elderly priest who was dying from an inoperable brain tumour. He spent the last days of his life unable to move but he clung onto his cross.

(c) Prayer beads

Prayer beads are another aid. Most people have heard of Catholic rosary beads with their repeated prayers and selected stories from the Gospels to be read and meditated upon. The petitions to the Virgin Mary are obviously not congenial to many Christians, but there are other forms of prayer beads around or that can be devised. There are also Eastern Orthodox prayer ropes, knotted lengths of rope upon which the Jesus Prayer is counted. The Jesus Prayer can take many forms. The longest form goes like this: "Lord Jesus Christ, Son of the living God, have mercy on me, a sinner." This can be shortened down to just "Jesus" or any number of variations.

The constant repetition of the same prayer makes some Christians wary. This sounds like the "vain repetitions" mentioned in the Sermon on the Mount (Matthew 6:7). These should not be used in this way, though. The repeated prayers are supposed to soak into the spirit, over and over again, rather like singing choruses any number of times to bask in their blessing.

You can use Scripture verses instead, such as parts of Psalm 23. It might be something to try, to see if it is helpful.

People are different, and these aids can help some but leave others switched off.

(d) Symbol of the resurrection
Finally, have a symbol of the resurrection somewhere around the house so that you will constantly be reminded of this great hope. You might use a decorated Scripture verse, an icon, a painting or something. Perhaps this is stuck on your fridge or placed in a quiet corner where you can also sit and pray.

It is also useful to place flowers and a card on a memorial shelf in a church, if there is one. This could be done on the anniversary of a death, each year.

Prayers and Services

Some find it helpful to arrange a requiem communion service to remember the deceased and to give thanks for their life. The beauty of doing this around communion is that the death and resurrection of Jesus are central, and sharing communion reminds us of the bread of life (John 6:54). It also reminds us that we are part of the communion of saints that death cannot break.

Litanies for the departed are offered in some churches but other Christians find any form of prayer for the dead disturbing. These prayers can be no more than a respectful remembrance of the departed before God, and prayers for those left behind.

Look at these prayers, extracted from the Eastern Orthodox Church, adapted from the Service Book of the Antiochian Orthodox Christian Archdiocese of North America:

Extracts from the Trisagion for the Dead

Holy God, Holy Mighty, Holy Immortal, have mercy on us.
Holy God, Holy Mighty, Holy Immortal, have mercy on us.
Holy God, Holy Mighty, Holy Immortal, have mercy on us.
Our Father

With the spirits of the righteous made perfect, give rest to
the soul of Your servant, ... , O Saviour; and preserve it in
that life of blessedness which is with You, O You who love
mankind.

In the place of Your rest, O Lord, where all your saints
repose, give rest also to the soul of Your servant... , for
You love mankind.

Glory to the Father, and to the Son, and to the Holy Spirit:
You are our God who descended into Hell and loosed the
bonds of those who were there. Yourself also give rest to
the soul of Your servant...

Have mercy on us, O God, according to Your great good-
ness, we pray. Hearken and have mercy.

Lord have mercy, Lord have mercy, Lord have mercy.

That the Lord God will establish his soul where the just
repose; the mercies of God, the kingdom of heaven, and
the remission of his sins, let us ask of Christ, our
Immortal King and our God.

The following is a suggestion for a small home service that
might be renewed each year upon the anniversary of the
departed's death, or held with close friends soon after
their crossing over.

- Gather in a quiet place, maybe at home, or in church,
  with a few close friends and/or family.
- Place a photograph of the deceased on a table.

- Light a candle.
- Read a passage from Scripture about the hope of heaven or the resurrection, maybe John 14:1–6.
- Place an object, a trinket, a symbol, of the departed on the table. Maybe each person present can do so. Share something about these.
- Place a decorated box on the table, wrapped as though it is an open present. Have each person pretend to take something from this. Share what gifts the departed gave to you – perhaps humour or love – or share a precious memory.
- Have a short time of open, free prayer, giving thanks for their life, and give thanks for the resurrection of Jesus.
- Have a time of silent reflection for all that the departed meant to you.
- Read 1 Thessalonians 4:16–18
- Say the Lord's Prayer and the Grace.

Keep it short and intimate. This is just enough, just enough.

"Let not your heart be troubled; you believe in God, believe also in Me. In My Father's house are many mansions; if it were not so, I would have told you. I go to prepare a place for you. And if I go and prepare a place for you, I will come again and receive you to Myself; that where I am, there you may be also. And where I go you know, and the way you know."

Thomas said to Him, "Lord, we do not know where You are going, and how can we know the way?"

Jesus said to him, "I am the way, the truth, and the life. No one comes to the Father except through Me."

(John 14:1–6)

Epilogue:
Sheltered by the Glory...

The London bombings of July 7 were devastating. Many lost their lives or were severely injured and traumatised. I was trying to get into London that day, amazingly, as I hardly ever take the trouble to travel into the City. I was stuck in chaos and closed stations before we knew what was going on. Thankfully, I did not know any of the victims, and friends of mine who were in London that day were safe.

A little later, during a time of worship, I had a strong sense of the presence of God and a mental picture of his mercy and glory, mercy and glory mixed, fused, married and intertwined. I had been reflecting upon the horror of the situation in the sections of the tube where the explosions happened. People lay mangled, torn from this life in an instant, shocked, surprised and bewildered. What would await them? How many of them had faith in this life? How many confessed Jesus Christ? I remember the description of one eyewitness, a journalist, who was in a carriage further away from the blast in one of the incidents. She was haunted by the screams of a dying man.

What I sensed, what I saw with the eyes of my spirit, was brilliant white light, the Glory of God. In the foreground this took the shape of an angelic figure with an overarching wing raised and sheltering those entering it. This spoke of the Psalms:

> He who dwells in the secret place of the Most High
> Shall abide under the shadow of the Almighty...
> He shall cover you with His feathers,
> And under His wings you shall take refuge.
>
> (Psalm 91:1, 4)

The Glory, the light, was also liquid, like cascading water, a waterfall of mercy. Various Scriptural images are conjured up here:

> His feet were like fine brass, as if refined in a furnace, and His voice as the sound of many waters. (Revelation 1:15)

> But the water that I shall give him will become in him a fountain of water springing up into eternal life.　　(John 4:14)

> And he showed me a pure river of water of life, clear as crystal, proceeding from the throne of God and of the Lamb.　　　　　　　(Revelation 22:1)

"Water of life"... It is hard to put what I sensed into words, but this playful, teasing image grasps it. "Water of life". The liquid Glory gave life and healing. Mercy poured down.

Then I sensed that those who had entered this were

washed from all their pain and they stood whole, free, healed, in the Glory. That is what awaited those who were cruelly torn from this life. That was the heart of God for them. I do not know how many confessed Jesus before they were killed. I do not know how many turned to him in those sacred seconds as they crossed over, saying "Yes" to his offer of life. They had the freedom to reject even then. Some might not have been able to see or hear. But this was the heart of God for them, and his glory would have burned brightly and blasted away defences of pride, fear and unbelief.

A little later I took the funeral of a young woman in her mid twenties who had tragically died, suffering from a terminal illness. She seemed to have no time for contact with the Church or faith. I don't know what was going inside her in those final months of her life. Many were praying for her, including some of her family. Powerful prayers, prayers of anointed men with healing ministries. When it came to her funeral, I had a number of our congregation praying for the mourners in the church vestry. It was a packed church, heavy with grief. I had a little prompt, a poke from the Holy Spirit. "Wear your wedding gear." This means some fine, long golden robes. I don't normally wear those for funerals. They are special ones for celebrations such as Christmas and Easter. This seemed a little strange, but I did so. Then I felt an urge to speak of the Glory that they symbolised. Somehow, I sensed that the young woman was in the hands of God and was in the healing, liquid Glory, covered in mercy. The "wedding gear" spoke of the Glory and of saying "Yes" to the "water of life".

I did not know it at the time, but one of the intercessors had a striking vision of the Glory of God falling over the coffin and angels rejoicing. Neither did I know that the deceased had struggled for the last hour or so of life and then had been overcome with an incredible peace and she settled into the well-known, big smile that she used to have. Then she died.

God had revealed His Glory and she had said "Yes". The moment of crossing over is holy ground, where we have an appointment with our Maker and he is in charge. It is not too late to say "Yes" at this point, but how much better it is if we seek the living God earlier in life. And the Scriptures warn us that some might become so hardened that they cannot turn, even when blasted with the Mercy and the Glory (c.f. John 3:19–21). That is tragic, indeed.

The time of crossing over is holy ground.